BISON
BOOKS

Extra Bases

Reflections on
Jackie Robinson,
Race, and
Baseball History

Jules Tygiel

University of
Nebraska Press
Lincoln and
London

Acknowledgments for the use of previously published
material appear on page 165, which constitutes
an extension of the copyright page.
© 2002 by the University of Nebraska Press

⊗

Library of Congress Cataloging-in-Publication Data
Tygiel, Jules.
Extra bases: reflections on Jackie Robinson,
race, and baseball history.
p. cm.
Includes bibliographical references.
ISBN 0-8032-9447-6 (pbk. : alk. paper)
1. Baseball—United States—History.
2. Discrimination in sports—United States.
3. Robinson, Jackie, 1919–1972.   4. United States—
Race relations.   I. Title Reflections on
Jackie Robinson, race, and baseball history.   II. Title.
GV863.A1 T93 2002
2002017975

In memory of G. Stanley and Violet Custer

Contents

Introduction

The turning points of one's life often arrive unannounced and unexpected. The two pivotal moments of my professional career occurred seventeen years and three thousand miles apart. The first took place in Brooklyn in 1956, when I was seven years old. My father, fulfilling his paternal obligations, escorted me to Ebbets Field for a night game between the Dodgers and the Philadelphia Phillies. Duke Snider and Gil Hodges hit solo home runs, but the Dodgers nonetheless trailed 5–2 heading into the bottom of the ninth inning. Then the miracle began. Jim Gilliam led off with a walk and Pee Wee Reese struck out. Snider strode to the plate and again launched a ball majestically over the right field fence onto Bedford Avenue to make the score 5–4. Randy Jackson, one of the lesser lights of the fabled Dodger teams of the 1950s, then drove a shot into the left field stands, tying the score. Hodges followed with his second home run of the night to send the Dodgers and their fans home as 6–5 victors. It is, in all probability, the only time in baseball history that a team had struck three consecutive homeruns in their final at bat to win a game. An impressionable seven-year-old boy had discovered the first great love in his life.

By 1973 I had matured into a twenty-four-year-old graduate student in history. Like the Dodgers, I now resided in Los Angeles, where I attended UCLA. Each day, I retreated to the same desk on the second floor of the University Research Library, where I studied for my upcoming doctoral examinations. On one occasion I found that someone had serendipitously left the 1947 volume of *Time* magazine on the table. My mind instantaneously reacted, as it often did to a date, with a baseball connection: "Nineteen forty-seven . . . Jackie Robinson." I thumbed through the lengthy tome, looking for a mention of Robinson's historic feat. He appeared, boldly and vibrantly on the cover of the September 22 issue, his ebony black face breaking through a sea of white baseballs. The story inside described his tumultuous first year and featured both well-known and long-forgotten details.

I turned ahead several weeks to read the letters written in response to the article. Some praised Robinson; others recoiled at his very image on the cover. It struck me that here was a tale at once familiar and yet unexplored. While sportswriters and baseball participants had written extensively about Robinson, historians had not. Robinson's saga had never been subjected to careful historical research, nor placed fully into the context of its time. I decided that someday I would combine my vocation as a historian with my avocation as a baseball fan in order to retell and reinterpret this tale.

The result was *Baseball's Great Experiment: Jackie Robinson and His Legacy*, published by Oxford University Press in 1983. When I wrote *Baseball's Great Experiment*, I did not (and still don't) consider myself a "baseball historian." My earlier research and writing had been on urban and labor history. I have subsequently published a book on an oil and stock swindle in Los Angeles in the 1920s. I like to think of myself as an American historian, who writes, among other things, about baseball. Nonetheless, the enduring power of the Jackie Robinson legend and the favorable reception accorded my first book propelled me into a new trajectory. As an established "expert" on Robinson, the Negro Leagues, and baseball history in general, I was invited to speak across the country and, more significantly, to write further on a wide variety of subjects related to baseball. In 2000 I returned to the national pastime as the subject of a book-length manuscript titled *Past Time: Baseball As History* (Oxford University Press).

During the seventeen years between the publication of these two books, I had written many pieces that reflected on and expanded on the themes I had introduced therein. The current collection brings these pieces together in one volume. These essays originated in a variety of formats. Most represent unsought solicitations: invitations to write for a journal or newspaper, a new encyclopedia on baseball history, or an introduction to the reissuing of a baseball classic. Some stemmed naturally from my previous research on Jackie Robinson, the Negro Leagues, and baseball integration. Others addressed more general areas of baseball and sports history. They appear here largely as originally written, though I have attempted to edit out repetition, and in one case I merged two related pieces and in another split a long essay into two shorter ones.

All of these articles, I believe, demonstrate the fundamental strategy I employ when writing about sports, one that distinguishes the work of the academic from that of the popular historian. I always, in effect, take my eye *off* the ball. As a fan, I focus primarily on what is happening on the field. As a historian, however, I am more interested in the broader cultural milieu that surrounds the game—how developments in the game of baseball reflect American society and the ways in which our nation has changed over time.

I have divided *Extra Bases* into three parts: "Reflections on Jackie Robinson," "Reflections on Race and Baseball," and "Reflections on Baseball History." The first part includes articles that I have written about Robinson subsequent to the publication of *Baseball's Great Experiment.* "The Court-Martial of Jackie Robinson" regards Robinson's turbulent military career as an example of the African-American experience in World War II. "Jackie Robinson's Signing: The Untold Story" is a collaboration with my fellow baseball historian, John Thorn, that includes new information about Branch Rickey and Jackie Robinson, and a reinterpretation of their relationship based on materials unearthed after the publication of my original research. The remaining two articles in this section were written in 1997 as part of the commemoration of the fiftieth anniversary of Jackie Robinson's major league debut. The first is a brief biographical sketch that served as the introduction to the *Jackie Robinson Reader,* a collection I edited for Dutton/Signet. The concluding piece was designed as an afterword to a new edition of *Baseball's Great Experiment,* discussing how Robinson's legacy had evolved over the half century since his historic breakthrough.

Part 2, "Reflections on Race and Baseball," includes "Black Ball," a lengthy essay on the history of African Americans and baseball that has appeared, regularly revised, in each of the seven editions of *Total Baseball.* I have divided it here into two distinct compositions. The first leads off this segment and describes the Negro Leagues and baseball's Jim Crow Era. The second discusses race relations in baseball since 1947. In addition, I have included two more works on the Negro Leagues. "Unreconciled Strivings," originally chapter 6 in *Past Time,* is the only piece that initially appeared in the first edition of one of my other books. I have included it here, however, because it complements the "Black Ball" article and rounds out my thinking on the Negro Leagues. It seemed a natural fit. The fourth selection is an introduction that I wrote for the University of Nebraska Press when they reissued Roy Campanella's autobiography *It's Good To Be Alive* as part of their series of classic baseball books. It looks not just at Campanella's career in the Negro Leagues and with the Dodgers, but at his life after the tragic automobile accident that ended his career and left him paralyzed.

Part 3, "Reflections on Baseball History," is a bit more eclectic and less finely focused. The first article is really a combination of two separate review essays that I wrote in 1986, one for the journal *Baseball History,* the other for the SABR REVIEW OF BOOKS. Both journals are now defunct, though hopefully not because of these contributions. The *Baseball History* piece discussed books about baseball written by academics in the 1980s, and the SABR article assessed the state of Negro League literature. I have merged them here into a lengthier analysis of what baseball history has to offer and how I believe it should be written. "Sports from a Sofa" is not about baseball per se, but it is a review of Ben Rader's book *In Its Own Image: How Television Has Changed Sports*. I include it as an example of my thinking on the intersection of television and baseball.

Baseball and television, of course, came together most completely in *Baseball*, Ken Burns's epic eighteen-hour documentary. While I enjoyed Burns's series, I also had reservations about it. The North American Society for Sport History (NASSH) invited me to participate in a panel discussion of *Baseball*, where I expressed these views. NASSH later published my remarks in its *Journal of Sport History* under the title "Ken Burns Meets Jackie Robinson." The selection on the Polo Grounds also resulted from an invitation. In 2001 Oxford University Press decided to honor Sheldon Meyer upon his retirement as their American history editor and asked a group of his authors to contribute articles describing places in the United States that revealed to them a slice of Americana. I naturally chose a baseball locale, the Polo Grounds, where as a teenager I had watched the New York Mets cavort. The piece captures both my own adventures and the broader history of the grand old ballpark. Unlike those that precede it, the final excerpt, "Salaries Are Escalating, but They Don't Guarantee Winning," represents a rare reflection (for me) on the current state of the game, though addressed, not surprisingly, from a historical perspective. It first appeared in the *Los Angeles Times* in the wake of the signing of Alex Rodriguez by the Texas Rangers for a quarter of a billion dollars.

I consider myself quite fortunate to have written these articles. It is a rare privilege to spend one's time writing about something that one enjoys so much. I am often amused that I have become a baseball "pundit," since many people's knowledge of the game, for example my colleagues in the Society for American Baseball Research (SABR), exceeds my own. Nonetheless, my primary contribution has been to apply the tools of the professional historian to the study of baseball, taking it seriously as a manifestation of American culture and treating it as a powerful window into the nation's past. I hope that readers, both those already familiar with my work and those who are experiencing it for the first time, will enjoy running a few extra bases with me and that the essays herein will inspire their own reflections on America, baseball, and history.

I
REFLECTIONS ON JACKIE ROBINSON

ONE

Introduction to *The Jackie Robinson Reader*

Extraordinary lives often reveal ordinary truths. Jackie Robinson was born in 1919 and died in 1972. He crammed into these brief fifty-three years a legacy of accomplishment, acclaim, controversy, and influence matched by few Americans. He was, even before his historic baseball breakthrough, an athlete of legendary proportions. He won fame and adulation as the first African-American to play in the major leagues in the twentieth century, launching an athletic revolution that transformed American sports. He garnered baseball's highest honors: Rookie of the Year, Most Valuable Player, and first-ballot election to the Hall of Fame. More significantly, Robinson became a symbol of racial integration and a prominent leader in the civil rights struggle of the 1950s and 1960s. Yet Jackie Robinson's half century among us illuminates not just the contours of an exceptional life, but much about the broader African-American experience of those years.

Jackie Robinson was born in Georgia in the heart of the segregated South, the grandson of a slave and the son of sharecrop farmers. While Jackie was still an infant, his father, Jerry Robinson, abandoned the family. His mother, Mallie, seeking a better life for Jackie and his four older siblings, joined the post–World War "great migration" of African Americans out of the South. Most blacks traveled to the eastern metropolises: New York, Philadelphia, Washington, or to Midwestern manufacturing centers like Chicago and Detroit. Mallie Robinson, on the advice of a brother, headed west to California.

African Americans were relatively rare in California in the 1920s. Although Mexican-born blacks had figured prominently in the early settlement of the region, by the early twentieth century blacks accounted for only 1 percent of the state's population. Those who lived there confronted a pattern of discrimination common to the American West. Although few laws addressed the issue of black-white relations, widely established and accepted practices defined the limits of tolerance. Few hotels, restaurants, or recreational facilities accepted African Americans. Restrictive covenants and other less formal practices barred blacks from living in most neighborhoods. Job discrimination impeded economic advancement. African Americans met hostility at almost every turn from strangers, neighbors, and police.

Thus Jackie Robinson grew up in an environment quite similar to that of other children of the great migration. Raised in a family without a father and sustained by their mother's income from domestic work—the most commonly available job for an African-American woman—the Robinsons lived in poverty, held together by their mother's indomitable spirit and strong sense of Methodist moralism. As a teenager in Pasadena, Robinson ran with local street gangs and experienced inevitable confrontations with the easily provoked local police, resulting in at least one arrest.

However, if southern California offered a harsh existence, it also proffered opportunities unavailable in most other locales. The absence of tenements and the predominance of single-family houses allowed Mallie Robinson to buy a home for her family. The lack of restrictions on black athletic participation opened an avenue of success to her sons. First, Jackie's older brother Mack, who starred at the University of Oregon and at the 1936 Olympic Games, and then Jackie, who won renown in four sports at Pasadena City College and UCLA, took advantage of this option.

Robinson's years at UCLA introduced him to high-level interracial competition. Unlike his later career, Robinson was not "the first" African-American athlete at UCLA. All-American Kenny Washington, like Robinson an extraordinary all-around athlete, who starred in football, baseball, and basketball, and future movie actor Woody Strode both preceded Robinson at UCLA. Robinson's childhood friend, Ray Bartlett, was the fourth black starter on the 1939 football team. While most black athletes of the era played for Negro colleges or in Negro Leagues and on clown teams like the Harlem Globetrotters, Robinson achieved his initial stardom on integrated playing fields.

Even more significantly, in his senior year at UCLA, Robinson met his future wife, Rachel Isum. Rachel, a freshman, was five years younger than Jackie, and came from a more secure black middle-class background. She was a third-generation Californian, a rare status among African Americans, had earned an academic scholarship to UCLA, and maintained a straight A average. Rachel's calm, warm, thoughtful manner complemented Jackie's fiery impetuousness. They formed an enduring bond of mutual love and support that would gird them through the challenging years ahead.

Like others of their generation, Jackie and Rachel found their courtship interrupted by World War II. Robinson's army career typified the African-American military experience. Drafted in April 1942 and assigned to Fort Riley, Kansas, Robinson ran an endless gauntlet of racial discrimination. He was barred from Officers' Candidate School, blocked from playing on the camp baseball team, and restricted to segregated facilities. Robinson, however, applied both his aggressiveness and celebrity to demand better treatment. He rose to the rank of lieutenant and waged a campaign to improve conditions for black soldiers at Fort Riley. After his transfer to Fort Hood in Texas, Robinson refused to move to the back of a military bus and defied the officers who attempted to discipline him, resulting in a court-martial that might have led to dishonorable discharge. A military tribunal acquitted Robinson of all charges, but the episode nonetheless left its mark and intensified Robinson's commitment to racial justice.

Upon his release from the army, Robinson faced a familiar dilemma for African Americans. Although at the peak of his athletic talents and good enough to star in any of the major American team sports, Robinson, like his brother Mack, and Kenny Washington before him, had few professional options. Neither organized baseball, the National Football League, nor most major basketball teams accepted black players. Robinson's best alternative was to cast his lot with baseball's Negro Leagues, and in the spring of 1945 he signed with the Kansas City Monarchs.

There can be little doubt that, at their best, the Negro Leagues played a high level of baseball, featuring some of the game's greatest stars. Robinson's own 1945 Monarch team included standout pitchers Satchel Paige and Hilton Smith. Opposing players included future Baseball Hall of Famers Buck Leonard, Josh Gibson, Roy Campanella, and Martin Dihigo. For Robinson, however, the Negro Leagues proved a distasteful experience. Accustomed to the highly structured training and scheduling of major college sports and hostile to all forms of segregation, Robinson considered the Negro Leagues a step down rather than a leg up. The long, hot bus rides through the South, the degrading treatment at gas stations and other white-owned facilities, and the players' own informal approach to most nonleague contests frustrated Robinson. An intensely private individual who neither smoked, drank, nor enjoyed what Paige called the "social ramble," Robinson never really fit in among the Monarchs. Although Robinson performed well with Kansas City, batting .387 and starting as shortstop in the East-West All-Star Game, and despite the fact that he gained invaluable training and exposure to top-flight baseball competition, Robinson, unlike most of his teammates and rivals, always disparaged his brief stint in the Negro Leagues.

Unbeknownst to Robinson, his performances with the Monarchs attracted intense scrutiny. Brooklyn Dodger president Branch Rickey had secretly decided to bring blacks into the major leagues and, under the guise of forming a new Brown Dodger squad, assigned his top scouts to evaluate Negro League talent. From the start, Robinson was high on Rickey's list of prospects. In April *Pittsburgh Courier* sportswriter Wendell Smith arranged a tryout with the Boston Red Sox for Robinson and two other Negro League stars. The Red Sox, who agreed to the audition in the face of local political pressure, never considered signing Robinson. Shortly thereafter, Rickey met with Smith and quizzed him about potential players for the Brown Dodgers. Smith, who might have suspected Rickey's true intentions, recommended Robinson.

Branch Rickey often offered conflicting reasons for his historic decision to desegregate baseball. At times he spoke of the need to eradicate the memory of a black college player whom he had coached in 1904 who had wept when barred from staying with his teammates at a Midwestern hotel. At others he expressed moral and religious concerns. Almost as frequently, he denied any noble intentions and invoked his desire to field the best possible team. "The Negroes will make us winners for years to come," he accurately predicted. In addition, he surely recognized that in attracting fans from New York City's growing African-American population and by fielding winning teams, he would boost Dodger attendance. A combination of these factors, and a desire to make a mark in history beyond the boundaries of baseball, motivated Rickey.

What is often forgotten in light of the unequivocal success of the Rickey-Robinson alliance are the extraordinary risks that Rickey assumed in signing Robinson. Although Rickey correctly perceived that integration would bring profits, most major league magnates believed that luring more blacks to the ballpark would, in the words of New York Yankee owner Larry MacPhail, "result in lessening the value of several major league franchises." While Rickey felt that fears of player opposition and fan violence were exaggerated, he could exert minimal control over these possibilities.

Furthermore, in selecting Jackie Robinson, Rickey took a great gamble. Although a seasoned athlete, Robinson had minimal baseball experience. Other than his five months with the Monarchs, Robinson had not played serious competitive baseball since leaving UCLA five years earlier. Few considered him the best player in the Negro Leagues. More ominously, Rickey– who had traveled to California and done extensive research on Robinson's background–was well aware of the athlete's tempestuous nature and capacity for controversy. "Jackie had a genius for getting into extracurricular scrapes," wrote one Los Angeles sportswriter. His problems in the army, also known to Rickey, reinforced this image. Rickey discounted many of these reports, noting that most of Robinson's difficulties stemmed from asserting his rights or in response to discrimination. If Robinson were white, Rickey reasoned, his aggressiveness, both on and off the field, would have been "praised to the skies." This behavior by an African American, however, was "offensive to some white people." Rickey believed that rather than offend whites, Robinson's racial pride and combativeness, if consciously curbed, would rally them to his cause.

Other elements of Robinson's history and personality appealed to Rickey. Robinson boasted a college education and had been an army officer. He was intelligent, articulate, and comfortable in the limelight. He had, unlike most Negro League players, extensive experience in high-level interracial competition. In addition, Robinson had the type of athletic skills that Rickey always admired in a ballplayer: speed (the only crucial skill that Rickey believed could not be taught), daring, and a fierce competitive drive.

Before signing Robinson, however, Rickey elicited a promise from the young African American. Regardless of the vile insults he might face from opposing players, fans, or off the field during his early years in baseball, Robinson would not respond. He would curb his naturally combative instincts and "turn the other cheek." Robinson, who fully understood and welcomed the magnitude of the challenge confronting him, readily agreed.

In February 1946 Jackie Robinson married Rachel Isum in a church wedding in Los Angeles. Shortly thereafter, they departed for spring training in Florida to launch "baseball's great experiment." The South that Jackie Robinson entered in 1946 was a land of rigid segregation, lynchings, and racial oppression, the dismantling of Jim Crow a seemingly distant dream. Two years later, President Harry S. Truman would order the desegregation of the armed forces. Eight years would pass before the U.S. Supreme Court would issue its landmark *Brown v. Board of Education* decision. Seventeen-year-old Martin Luther King, Jr., was attending classes at Morehouse College. Robinson thus became what one writer has called "a one man civil rights movement."

From the moment of their arrival in Florida, the Robinsons encountered the specter of Jim Crow. In Pensacola, airline officials removed them from their scheduled flight. At Sanford, threats of violence forced Jackie and Rachel out of town. In Jacksonville and Deland, public officials refused to allow him to play. On one occasion a local sheriff paraded onto the field and demanded Robinson's ouster in mid-game. Yet Robinson, assigned to the Montreal Royals of the International League, the Dodgers' top farm club, participated freely in games at the Dodger home base in Daytona Beach and fans, both black and white, greeted his appearances enthusiastically. Local business leaders in many Florida communities, cognizant of the profits and publicity generated by baseball training camps, courted the integrated Dodgers for future seasons. While Rickey would shy away from bringing Robinson and the Dodgers back to Florida in 1947, Robinson had established an important precedent. Within just three years, cities throughout Florida and the rest of the South would clamor to host the Jackie Robinson Dodgers.

Throughout the ensuing 1946 season, Robinson, in the words of *New York Amsterdam News* columnist Joe Bostic, "ascended the heights of excellence to prove the rightness of the experiment. And prove it in the only correct crucible for such an experiment—the crucible of white hot competition." In the Royals' opening game at Jersey City, Robinson unveiled his charismatic ability to convert challenges into transcendent moments. The Montreal second baseman garnered four hits, including a three-run home run, scored four times, stole two bases, and twice scored from third by inducing the opposing pitcher to balk.

This extraordinary debut proved a prologue for an equally remarkable season. Despite a rash of brushback pitches, spiking attempts, threats of race riots in Baltimore (the league's southern-most city), and vile harassment by opposing players, Robinson led the International League in batting average (.349) and in runs scored (113). He finished second in stolen bases and registered the highest fielding percentage of any second baseman. Behind Robinson's inspirational play, Montreal won the league pennant by nineteen and a half games, returning to the South to meet, and ultimately defeat, the Louisville Colonels in the Little World Series for the championship of the minor leagues.

Robinson's spectacular season at Montreal dispelled most doubts about his right to play in the major leagues. Branch Rickey, however, kept Robinson on the Royals roster throughout spring training in 1947. Rickey had embarked on several strategems that he hoped would ease Robinson's way onto the Dodgers. He avoided the pitfalls of Florida segregation by dispatching the Dodgers and Royals to Cuba and Panama. He transformed Robinson into a first baseman, the Brooklyn club's greatest need. Rickey believed that a demonstration of Robinson's undeniable skills would generate a groundswell of support for his promotion among the Dodger players.

Robinson responded with a .429 spring batting tear, but rather than demand his ascension, several Dodgers, led by Alabama-born Dixie Walker, circulated a petition to keep him off the team. Several key players, however, most notably Kentucky-born shortstop Pee Wee Reese, refused to sign the protest and Rickey and manager Leo Durocher quickly quelled the rebellion. On April 10, five days before the start of the season, with no groundswell yet in sight, Rickey simply elevated Robinson to the parent club as the Dodger first baseman.

Around the National League, Robinson's arrival prompted undercurrents of dismay. The Philadelphia Phillies, under the leadership of manager Ben Chapman, subjected Robinson to an unconscionable stream of racial abuse. Rumors circulated that the St. Louis Cardinals and Chicago Cubs would strike rather than compete against a black player. Opposing pitchers targeted Robinson regularly with brushback and beanball pitches, hitting him a league-leading seven times in the first half of the season. Hotels in Philadelphia and St. Louis barred Robinson; in Cincinnati the hotel compelled him to take his meals in his room for fear his presence might offend other guests.

Amidst this backdrop of pressure and challenge, Robinson carved out not just an extraordinary rookie season, but a monument to courage and equal opportunity. After an early slump, Robinson relentlessly removed any remaining justifications for the exclusion of blacks in baseball. Robinson batted over .300 for most of the season. He led the league in stolen bases and trailed just one other player in runs scored. He paced the Dodgers in home runs and led them to the pennant. The *Sporting News*, which had consistently opposed the inclusion of blacks in organized baseball, awarded him its Rookie of the Year Award.

Yet Robinson's statistics and honors, impressive as they were, failed to capture his achievement. By injecting the more aggressive and flamboyant baserunning and batting styles of the Negro Leagues, Robinson transformed major league baseball. In the process, Robinson transformed the nation's consciousness as well.

Robinson had begun the 1947 season as a curiosity; he emerged as a national phenomenon. Wherever the Dodgers played, fans turned out in record numbers to witness the integration spectacle. Robinson doubtless benefited from the liberalized racial attitudes that had emerged during the Great Depression and World War II, but he simultaneously helped to forge a new consciousness that would accelerate the civil rights movement of the 1950s. African Americans saw Robinson as their standard-bearer leading the onslaught against segregation. Whites confronted in Robinson an individual who not only won their admiration as an athlete, but as a man, compelling them to reassess their views of both African Americans and American race relations.

Although few people realized it at the time, Robinson had also launched a revolution in American athletics. Only two other major league teams signed African-American players in 1947, and the pace of integration, in retrospect, seems agonizingly slow. Yet within a decade, blacks from the United States and Caribbean countries appeared on all but one team and had emerged as the dominant stars of the game. This pattern proved even more pronounced in other team sports. By the late 1960s, African Americans predominated in the National Football League and National Basketball Association. The black influx in college football and basketball forced Southern universities to first abandon policies barring competition against integrated squads and ultimately to recruit African Americans themselves. Sports became the primary symbol of social mobility in the black community, prompting concern about an overemphasis on athletics among African-American youth.

In the wake of his triumphant rookie season, Robinson transcended baseball and sports to become an American icon. Both on and off the field Robinson symbolized the promise of integration and equal opportunity. Numerous articles profiled not just Robinson the ballplayer, but the Robinson family, with Jackie and Rachel living in integrated neighborhoods, their children attending predominantly white schools, vanguards of the new racial enlightenment. As the nation's foremost representative of impending interracial improvement, Robinson found himself embroiled in 1949 in a cold war confrontation with singer-actor Paul Robeson, whose more pessimistic assessment of American race relations led him to an ill-fated flirtation with Soviet communism.

Robinson's dynamic play for the Dodgers reinforced his charismatic appeal. In 1949 Robinson led the National League in hitting, winning the Most Valuable Player Award, and began a string of six consecutive All-Star Game appearances. With the addition of catcher Roy Campanella, pitcher Don Newcombe, and other former Negro League stars, the Dodgers continued to showcase the benefits of integration. Equally important was the fact that Robinson, the proud, fierce, African-American firebrand, was clearly the leader and dominant personality on the National League's most accomplished and celebrated squad.

Yet amidst these growing achievements, Robinson's "genius for getting into extracurricular scrapes" reasserted itself. Upon signing with the Dodgers in 1945, Robinson had guaranteed Branch Rickey that he would ignore insults and assaults during the experimental phase of his career. By 1949 both Rickey and Robinson agreed that this chapter had ended. Robinson no longer needed to unnaturally restrain his responses to opposing players or anyone else.

The "new" Robinson seemed forever surrounded by a swirl of controversy. He complained that some umpires had it in for him. He warred with Giants manager Leo Durocher. He objected to the failure of the Yankees to sign black players, protested the continuing discrimination faced by black athletes in spring training, and demanded that blacks be considered as managers. His unrepentant outspokenness and civil rights militancy alternately attracted criticism and acclaim both inside and outside of baseball.

In January 1957, after ten tempestuous seasons, Jackie Robinson retired as a player. It is fitting testimony to his baseball prowess that his career record alone, without any consideration of his pioneering social role, merited his first-ballot election to the Hall of Fame five years later. His lifetime batting average was .311. His .410 on-base percentage ranks among the top twenty-five players of all time. The Dodgers won pennants in six of Robinson's ten years with the club and finished second three times. In addition, the color line had likely robbed Robinson, already twenty-eight years old when he joined the Dodgers, of at least five years of prime productivity.

Unlike most athletes, Robinson never retreated from the public eye after his retirement. He accepted a job as vice president of Chock Full O' Nuts, a chain of New York City fast-food restaurants that employed many African Americans. He chaired the NAACP Freedom Fund Drive and became one of that organization's primary spokespersons and fundraisers. He immersed himself in the civil rights movement as an ardent supporter of the Reverend Martin Luther King, Jr., raised funds for the Student Non-Violent Coordinating Committee (SNCC), and marched in many of the signpost demonstrations of the 1960s.

Yet Robinson also became engulfed in the turbulently shifting racial and generational tides of that decade. Always defiantly independent in thought and action, Robinson forged his own distinctive and controversial path in politics and protest. In 1960 he endorsed Richard Nixon for president over John F. Kennedy, the favorite of most civil rights activists. Although the vast majority of African Americans supported the Democrats, Robinson allied with New York Governor Nelson Rockefeller and became the nation's most prominent black Republican. As white and black radicals increasingly attacked the American economic and political system, Robinson reaffirmed his faith in "black capitalism" as the vehicle for African-American progress, establishing the Freedom National Bank and other black-owned enterprises.

In 1960 young SNCC activists successfully approached Robinson for assistance, seeing him as a kindred spirit. By the late 1960s, however, Robinson had publicly feuded with Malcolm X and subsequent black power advocates and split with Martin Luther King, Jr., over King's opposition to the Vietnam War. Indeed, Robinson came to be regarded by many militants as a pillar of the mainstream establishment; in some quarters as an Uncle Tom. Ironically, these attacks coincided with Robinson's resignation from the NAACP as a result of its domination by a "clique of the Old Guard" and failure to incorporate "younger, more progressive voices."

Accustomed to contention, Robinson could confidently navigate these controversies. Personal tragedy, however, took a far deeper toll. On March 6, 1968, police arrested twenty-one-year-old Jackie Jr., recently returned from Vietnam where he had been wounded in action, for possession of drugs and a firearm. Where Jackie Sr. had been a herald of the "New Negro" of the civil rights movement, his son became a harbinger of the devastation that would decimate African-American males in the 1980s and 1990s. Addicted to heroin in Vietnam, the younger Robinson had turned to a life of crime. Jackie Jr. entered Daytop Village, a Staten Island drug rehabilitation center. He emerged cured of his addiction and devoted to helping others afflicted by drugs. Fate would allow him little time to savor his triumph. In the early morning hours of June 17, 1971, the sports car he was driving veered out of control and crashed on the Merritt Parkway near the Robinson home in Connecticut, killing twenty-four-year-old Jackie Robinson, Jr.

His son's ordeal and death transformed the elder Robinson. The tragedy had been played out, as had most of his adult life, in public view. "I guess I had more of an effect on other people's kids than I had on my own," rued Robinson after Jackie Jr.'s arrest, as unsparing in his self-criticism as in his attacks on others. Robinson's physical condition declined precipitously. Plagued for a decade with diabetes, Robinson found his eyesight failing. He suffered a heart attack, and poor blood circulation made it difficult for him to walk. The amputation of his left leg grew imminent. In addition, coming closely on the heels of the 1968 King assassination and election of Richard Nixon, with whom Robinson had long since parted company, the trials of Jackie Jr. led Robinson, like many other African Americans, to reevaluate his faith in America's ability to overcome its history of racism and discrimination.

This reassessment culminated in the 1972 publication of Robinson's remarkable final testament, his bluntly titled autobiography *I Never Had It Made*. Robinson remained characteristically frank and outspoken. He expressed pride in his accomplishments, but nonetheless acknowledged where he had erred—in his castigation of Robeson, his endorsement of Nixon, his split with King over Vietnam, and other episodes. He wrote honestly and movingly about Jackie Jr. Most tellingly, Robinson, who for a quarter of a century had symbolized the possibility of integration in America, now sounded a profoundly pessimistic note. "There was a time I believed deeply in America. I have become bitterly disillusioned," he wrote. Although he acknowledged that "Personally, I have been very fortunate. . . . I cannot say I have it made while our country . . . speeds along a course toward more and more racism."

Yet the image of Robinson in his final years as broken and dispirited belies the reality of his indomitable personality. The publication of Roger Kahn's *The Boys of Summer* in 1971 reawakened a new generation to the power and the glory of the Robinson saga. Those who saw and spoke to Robinson in 1972 describe him as ever ebullient and optimistic, despite his personal grief and physical difficulties. Kahn, in a final telephone conversation, found Robinson "as enthusiastic as a twenty-year-old" in discussing his latest business venture. When major league baseball, at the 1972 World Series, chose to honor the twenty-fifth anniversary of Robinson's debut, he joked with his former teammates about his impending amputation, needling Pee Wee Reese that he would return to best him on the golf course. Then before a national television audience Robinson offered America one final enduring memory. After accepting the accolades of the dignitaries, he challenged organized baseball to fulfill his legacy by hiring black managers.

Nine days later, on October 24, 1972, Robinson died of a heart attack. He was only fifty-three years old. For the eulogy Rachel Robinson, who had shared Jackie's triumphs and heartbreaks, chose not someone from Robinson's baseball past, nor one of his long-standing allies from earlier civil rights struggles, but thirty-one-year-old Reverend Jesse Jackson, an African-American leader who embodied the hopes of the future rather than the disappointments of the past.

Jesse Jackson, like Rachel Robinson, understood Robinson's true final testament. Robinson, preached Jackson, had "created ripples of possibility," "turned stumbling block into stepping stone," and bequeathed the "gift of new expectations." In his autobiography Robinson had vented his disappointment with the state of race relations in the 1970s, but he also reaffirmed the message that has made him such an enduring figure: That individuals of courage and commitment can confront bigotry and create change. In *I Never Had It Made*, Robinson had tempered his disillusionment with a far more uplifting epitaph: "A life is not important except in the impact it has on other lives." By that measure, one quarter century after his death and one half century after his historic feat, the import of Jackie Robinson's life continues to resound.

TWO

The Court-Martial of Jackie Robinson

On July 6, 1944, Jackie Robinson, a twenty-five-year-old lieutenant, boarded an Army bus at Fort Hood, Texas. Sixteen months later he would be tapped as the man to break baseball's color barrier, but in 1944 he was one of thousands of blacks thrust into the Jim Crow South during World War II. He was with the light-skinned wife of a fellow black officer, and the two walked half the length of the bus, then sat down, talking amiably. The driver, gazing into his rearview mirror, saw a black officer seated in the middle of the bus next to a woman who appeared to be white. "Hey, you, sittin' beside that woman," he yelled. "Get to the back of the bus."

Lieutenant Robinson ignored the order. The driver stopped the bus, marched back to where the two passengers were sitting, and demanded that the lieutenant "get to the back of the bus where the colored people belong." Robinson refused, and so began a series of events that led to his arrest and court-martial and, finally, threatened his entire career.

Jackie Robinson was already a national celebrity in 1944. During a spectacular athletic career at the University of California at Los Angeles, he had starred in basketball, football, track, and baseball. He was drafted in April 1942, and during the following year a study of blacks in the Army singled him out. "Social intercourse between the races has been discouraged," it was reported in *Jim Crow Joins Up*, "yet Negro athletes such as Joe Louis, the prizefighter, and Jack Robinson, the All-American football star . . . are today greatly admired in the army."

Initially, Robinson had been assigned to a cavalry unit at Fort Riley, Kansas, where he applied for Officers' Candidate School. Official Army policy provided for the training of black officers in integrated facilities; in reality, however, few blacks had yet gained access to ocs. At Fort Riley, Robinson was rejected and told, off the record, that blacks were excluded from ocs because they lacked leadership ability.

Robinson took his plight not to Army officials but to an even more commanding figure—Joe Louis, the heavyweight boxing champion of the world. Louis was also stationed at Fort Riley, and although he was not a commissioned officer, his status was somewhat higher than that of a raw recruit. Louis investigated the situation and arranged a meeting for black soldiers to voice their grievances in the presence of a representative of the secretary of war. Within a few days of this session, several blacks, including Robinson, were enrolled in ocs.

Robinson's Army career, however, continued to be stormy, and a good part of the tempest revolved around sports. Athletics were an important part of military life; teams from different Army forts competed against one another and against college teams. Professional and college athletes, once drafted, often found themselves spending the war on the baseball diamond or the gridiron. The coaches of Fort Riley's highly competitive football team tried to persuade Robinson—at the time more renowned for his football prowess than for his baseball skills—to join the squad.

Robinson had other ideas. Earlier in his Army career he had wanted to try out for the camp baseball team. Pete Reiser, who was to be Robinson's teammate on the Dodgers and who played on the Fort Riley squad, later recalled Robinson's humiliating rejection: "One day a Negro lieutenant came out for the ball team. An officer told him he couldn't play. 'You have to play for the colored team,' the officer said. That was a joke. There was no colored team. The lieutenant stood there for a while watching us work out. Then he turned and walked away. I didn't know who he was then, but that was the first time I saw Jackie Robinson. I can still remember him walking away by himself."

Refused the baseball field, Robinson balked at representing Fort Riley as a running back. A colonel threatened to order him to participate, but Robinson remained adamant. To the dismay of the Fort Riley football fans, the best running back in camp refused to suit up.

In January 1943 Robinson was commissioned a second lieutenant and appointed acting morale officer for a black company at Fort Riley. As might be expected, the principal obstacles to high morale were the Jim Crow regulations governing the camp. Particularly upsetting were conditions at the post exchange, where only a few seats had been set aside for black soldiers. Robinson telephoned the base provost marshal, Major Hafner, to protest this situation; the major said that taking seats away from the white soldiers and giving them to black would cause a problem among the white troops. Furthermore, he could not believe that the lieutenant actually wanted the races seated together.

"Let me put it this way," Robinson remembered the officer as saying: "How would you like to have your wife sitting next to a nigger?"

Robinson exploded. "Major, I happen to be a Negro," he shouted, "and I don't know that to have anyone's wife sitting next to a Negro is any worse than to have her sitting next to some of these white soldiers I see around here."

"I just want you to know," said Hafner, "that I don't want my wife sitting close to any colored guy."

"How the hell do you know that your wife hasn't already been close to one?" asked Robinson as he launched into a tirade against the major.

The provost marshal hung up on him, but Robinson's protest was not fruitless: although separate areas in the post exchange remained the rule, blacks were allotted additional seats.

Robinson was never punished or disciplined for being insolent to his superior officer, but he was soon transferred to the 761st Tank Battalion at Fort Hood, Texas. It was not an improvement. "The prejudice and discrimination at Camp Hood made [other bases] seem ultraliberal in [their] attitude," recalled Harry Duplessis, one of Robinson's fellow black officers. "Camp Hood was frightening. . . . Segregation there was so complete that I even saw outhouses marked White, Colored, and Mexican."

Nevertheless, Robinson's performance was so outstanding that even though he was on "limited service" because of an old ankle injury, his commanding officer requested that he go overseas with the battalion. In order to do so, Robinson was required to sign a waiver relieving the Army of all responsibility in the event of injury. Robinson agreed, but Army medical authorities insisted the ankle be examined before giving their approval.

The medical examination took place at a hospital thirty miles from Fort Hood. While waiting for the results, Robinson got a pass to visit with his company. He arrived at the base to find the battalion off on maneuvers, so he stopped at the officers' club, where he met Mrs. Gordon H. Jones, the wife of another black lieutenant. Since she lived on the way to the hospital, they boarded the bus together.

For black soldiers in the South, the shortest bus trip could be a humiliating and even dangerous experience. According to the *Pittsburgh Courier*, which cited a "mountain of complaints from Negro soldiers," "frustrations on buses in the South was one of the most fruitful sources of trouble for Negro soldiers." In Durham, North Carolina, only weeks before, an altercation had ended with the driver shooting and killing a black soldier who had refused to move to the back of a bus. The driver was tried and found not guilty by a civilian jury. Unable to change the rules on civilian bus lines, the Army began to provide its own, nonsegregated buses on Southern bases. The action was given no publicity at first and was ignored at many bases. In June 1944, however, the story had been made public, and the resulting furor had brought the Army policy to the attention of many black soldiers.

When Robinson boarded the bus with Mrs. Jones on July 6, he was aware that military buses had been ordered desegregated. As he wrote to the National Association for the Advancement of Colored People (NAACP) two weeks later, "I refused to move because I recalled a letter from Washington which states that there is to be no segregation on army posts." In his autobiography Robinson stated that the boxers Joe Louis and Ray Robinson had also influenced his actions by their recent refusals to obey Jim Crow regulations at a bus depot in Alabama. In any event, Lieutenant Robinson told the driver: "The Army recently issued orders that there is to be no more racial segregation on any Army post. This is an Army bus operating on an Army post."

The man backed down, but at the end of the line, as Robinson and Mrs. Jones waited for a second bus, he returned with his dispatcher and two other drivers. The dispatcher turned to the driver and asked, "Is this the nigger that's been causing you trouble?" Leaving Mrs. Jones, Robinson shook a finger in the driver's face and told him to "quit f——— with me." As Robinson started walking away, two military policemen arrived on the scene and suggested that he explain the situation to the provost marshal.

Lieutenant Robinson was driven to military police headquarters by two MPs. They were met there by Pvt. Ben W. Mucklerath, who asked Cpl. George A. Elwood, one of ten MPs, if he had a "nigger lieutenant" in the car. Robinson told the enlisted man that "if he ever called me nigger again I would break him in two." The first officer on the scene was Capt. Peelor Wigginton, the officer of the day. When Wigginton began to take Mucklerath's story, Robinson interrupted. He was ordered out of the room until the assistant provost marshal, Capt. Gerald M. Bear, came to take over the investigation.

When the Southern-born Captain Bear arrived, Robinson started to follow him into the guard room, only to be told, "Nobody comes into the room until I tell him." Why then, asked Robinson, was Private Mucklerath already in the room? When Captain Wigginton began briefing Captain Bear on Mucklerath's testimony, Robinson, standing by the door, complained that the account was inaccurate.

The hostility grew with the arrival of a civilian woman named Wilson who was to record Robinson's statement. Robinson later recalled that the stenographer continually interrupted his statement with her own questions and comments, such as, "Don't you know you have no right sitting up there in the white part of the bus." Robinson challenged the right of a Texas civilian to interrogate him and finally snapped at her to stop interrupting. Captain Bear growled something about his being "uppity," and when Robinson insisted on making corrections in the written statement before signing it, the civilian stenographer jumped up and said, "I don't have to take that sassy kind of talk from you."

As a result of the evening's events, camp officials were determined to court-martial Robinson. When his commanding officer, Col. R. L. Bates, refused to endorse the court-martial orders, the authorities transferred Robinson to the 758th Tank Battalion, whose commander promptly signed. Robinson was charged with insubordination, disturbing the peace, drunkenness, conduct unbecoming an officer, insulting a civilian woman, and refusing to obey the lawful orders of a superior officer.

Faced with so many counts, Robinson feared that there was a conspiracy against him at Fort Hood and that he would be dishonorably discharged. He wrote to the NAACP for "advice or help on the matter."

"The people have a pretty good bunch of lies," he reported. "When I read some of the statements of the witnesses I was certain that these people had got together and was going to frame me." While admitting that he had cursed after the bus dispatcher had called him a "nigger," he denied "calling the people around all sorts of names." "If I didn't respect them," he protested, "I certainly would have Mrs. Jones."

Robinson was particularly upset because officials had not even asked Mrs. Jones to give a statement. He felt that he was "being unfairly punished because I wouldn't be pushed around by the driver of the bus," and was "looking for a civilian lawyer to handle my case because I know he will be able to free the truth with a little technique."

His fear of a conspiracy was not groundless. During World War II, according to the historian Jack D. Foner, "many black soldiers were unjustly convicted by courts-martial, either because their officers assumed their guilt regardless of the evidence or because they wanted to 'set an example' for other black soldiers." The demand on the NAACP for assistance for black soldiers was so great that they had to turn down most requests unless the case was deemed to be "of national importance to the Negro race." In a letter actually dated one day after the trial, the NAACP informed Robinson that "we will be unable to furnish you with an attorney in the event that you are court-martialled."

Meanwhile, among black soldiers in the Southwest, "Jackie Robinson's encounter with a cracker bus driver" had become, according to Lieutenant Duplessis, the "racial cause célèbre." Robinson's hasty transfer from the 761st Tank Battalion to the 758th led many black officers to believe that the Army was attempting to try him in secrecy. A group of them wrote letters to the NAACP and to two of the more influential black newspapers, the *Pittsburgh Courier* and the *Chicago Defender*. Lt. Ivan Harrison recalls the campaign as follows: "The NAACP, his fraternity, and the Negro press soon learned about Jackie and the messages began to pour in demanding to know what happened. They moved Jackie to another camp, then answered he was no longer a member of the 761st. Of course, the black underground soon notified them where he could be found. . . . It was beginning to be such a hot potato that they held what I am sure was the shortest court-martial in the history of the armed services."

Harrison was wrong about that; the court-martial proceedings lasted more than four hours. And although the black press made scant mention of the Robinson case, the officers' campaign did have some notable success. All charges stemming from the actual incident on the bus and Robinson's argument with the civilian secretary were dropped. He had still to face a court-martial, but on the two lesser charges of insubordination arising from his confrontation in the guardhouse.

Although the dismissal of the more serious charges was to Robinson's advantage, it also made his defense more difficult. He was being tried for insubordination, but no mention of the event which caused this rebellious behavior—the encounter on the bus—was to be allowed. Nor were the actions of the stenographer to be considered. Robinson was no longer on trial for refusing to move to the back of a bus, which was within his rights, or for responding to the racial slurs of a civilian, but for acting with "disrespect" toward Captain Bear and disobeying a lawful command given by that officer.

In the meantime, a problem had arisen regarding Robinson's defense. Unable to get help from the NAACP, he had been assigned a young Southern lawyer to act as his counsel. Before Robinson could even protest, the lawyer withdrew from the case: having been raised in the South, he said, he had not "developed arguments against segregation" that were necessary to defend Robinson adequately. He did, however, arrange for Robinson to engage Lt. William Cline, a lawyer from the Midwest who was eager to handle the case.

The court-martial of 2d Lt. Jackie Robinson took place on August 2, 1944. The heart of the prosecution's case was presented by Captains Bear and Wigginton, who told essentially the same story. As they had attempted to ascertain the facts of the events of July 6, Robinson continually interrupted them and acted disrespectfully. When ordered from the room, according to Bear, Robinson continued to stand by the half-gate door, "leaning on the half gate down in a slouching position with his elbows resting on the gate, and he kept interrupting." Several times, said Bear, he told the black lieutenant to get away from the door, and in response, Robinson bowed and said, "O.K., sir. O.K., sir. O.K., sir." Bear demonstrated the way in which Robinson bowed as he "kind of smirked or grimaced his face."

Captain Bear testified that he gave Robinson a direct order to remain seated until called upon. Instead the lieutenant went outside and was "pitching rocks" and talking to the driver of a jeep. When ordered back inside, said Bear, Robinson complied "reluctantly . . . with his hands in his pockets, swaying, shifting his weight from one foot to the other."

When Robinson was brought into the orderly room to make his statement, said Bear, "everything he said seemed facetious to him, and he seemed to be trying to make fun of it . . . he would raise and lower his words, and he would say, 'Oh, yeah' when I would ask him a question, and several times I asked him not to go so fast and to tone his language down." He seemed "argumentative" and asked questions such as, "Well, do I have to answer that?" When asked to speak more slowly, according to Bear, Robinson began to "baby talk," exaggerating the pause between each word.

Once Robinson's statement had been taken, Bear arranged transportation for him back to the hospital, but the lieutenant stated that he did not want to go back, since he had a pass until eight in the morning. In Captain Wigginton's opinion, Robinson was "very disrespectful," which led the officer of the day to threaten to arrest him for insubordination.

In his own testimony Robinson countered most of the accusations against him. He admitted breaking in on the conversation between Captain Wigginton and Private Mucklerath, but "to my mind I was not interrupting at all; Pvt. Mucklerath stated something that I did not think was quite right and I interrupted him to see if I could . . . get him to correct his statement." After complaining that Mucklerath had called him a "nigger lieutenant," he was asked if he knew what a nigger was. "I looked it up once," said Robinson, "but my grandmother gave me a good definition, she was a slave, and she said the definition of the word was a low, uncouth person, and pertains to no one in particular; but I don't consider that I am low and uncouth. . . . When I made this statement I did not like to be called nigger, I told the Captain, I said, 'If you call me a nigger, I might have said the same thing to you. . . .' I do not consider myself a nigger at all. I am a Negro, but not a nigger."

Robinson denied most of the specific accusations made against him and stated that Bear had been "not polite at all" from the moment he arrived, and "very uncivil toward me" when taking the statement. "He did not seem to recognize me as an officer at all. But I did consider myself an officer and felt that I should be addressed as one." And, he added bitterly, "they asked that private to sit down."

Robinson's testimony held up better under cross-examination than did Bear's or Wigginton's. There were several flaws and omissions in the accounts of the two captains. Referring to the "argumentative" questions Robinson had raised in giving his statement, Cline asked Bear if it was "improper for an accused to make such inquiry as that." When prodded, Bear stated that it was not. Had not Bear ordered Robinson to "be at ease," asked one of the judges presiding. If so, he continued, "I do not see the manner in which he leaned on the gate had anything to do with you."

The questions of whether Robinson had been placed under arrest on July 6 and whether he had refused to accept the transportation that Bear had ordered for his return to the hospital were also targets of the cross-examination. Defense questioning revealed that the vehicle provided was, in reality, a military police pickup truck. Yet Bear had testified that he had informed Robinson that he was being placed under arrest in quarters, in which case, no bodily restrictions were allowed. Robinson was within his rights to protest.

Lieutenant Cline was not totally successful in discrediting the witnesses for the prosecution. Efforts to relate Robinson's behavior to the incident on the bus were disallowed. Both Bear and Wigginton denied that there had been any unusual exchange between Robinson and the stenographer, preventing the defense from exploring this aspect of the case. Nonetheless, by the time the two men left the witness stand, key segments of their testimony had been either repudiated or placed in doubt.

The prosecution's cross-examination of Lieutenant Robinson was far less effective. Robinson denied having had any drinks that evening, though "evidently they thought I had." He also stated that he had not willfully disobeyed a direct order. The only reason that he had argued with Bear, he explained, was that he had asked the captain half a dozen times whether he was under arrest—and if he was not, Robinson wanted to know why he was being escorted back to the hospital under guard. By his own admission,

Bear had given Robinson ambiguous answers. Unlike Bear and Wigginton, Robinson was subjected to virtually no examination by the court-martial board.

The defense also presented several character witnesses from Robinson's battalion. The most significant testimony came from Colonel Bates. Bates stated that Robinson was an officer he would like to have under his command in combat, and several times the prosecution and the court itself reprimanded the colonel for volunteering unsolicited praise of Robinson.

When the defense had rested, the prosecution called a few additional witnesses. All supported the story told by Captains Bear and Wigginton but none proved to be particularly effective. Private Mucklerath was notably lacking in credibility. While he recalled Robinson's vow that if the private ever "called him a nigger he would break [me] in two," he denied having used that term and could not explain why the black lieutenant had said this. He was followed to the stand, however, by Corporal Elwood, who, while generally supporting the testimony of the other whites, admitted that Mucklerath had indeed asked him if he had a "nigger lieutenant" in the car.

Elwood was the last witness to be heard. The attorneys then made their closing arguments, and Robinson later recalled: "My lawyer summed up the case beautifully by telling the board that this was not a case involving any violation of the Articles of War, or even of military tradition, but simply a situation in which a few individuals sought to vent their bigotry on a Negro they considered 'uppity' because he had the audacity to exercise rights that belonged to him as an American and a soldier."

Robinson and his lawyer then settled down to await the verdict. They did not have long to wait. Voting by secret written ballot, the nine judges found Robinson "not guilty of all specifications and charges."

The ordeal that had begun almost a month earlier on a military bus was finally over. To some extent the acquittal was due to the fact that Robinson was a renowned figure—his conviction might have proven an embarrassment for the Army. For most other black soldiers, however, neither military nor Southern justice was likely to have produced such a conclusion.

Robinson was now free to resume his service career, but his Army experiences had taken their toll on his patriotic fervor. A month earlier he had been willing to waive his rights to compensation for injury and go overseas, but now his main desire was to leave the service altogether. With Colonel Bates and his tank battalion already on the way to Europe, Robinson did not wish to join another unit. He asked to be released from the Army. He was quickly transferred to Camp Breckinridge, Kentucky, where he coached black athletic teams until he was honorably discharged in November 1944.

Had the court-martial of Jackie Robinson been an isolated incident, it would be little more than a curious episode in the life of a great athlete. His humiliating confrontations with discrimination, however, were typical of the experience of the black soldier; and his rebellion against Jim Crow attitudes was just one of the many instances in which blacks, recruited to fight a war against racism in Europe, began to resist the dictates of segregation in America. As Robinson later wrote of his acquittal at Fort Hood, "It was a small victory, for I had learned that I was in two wars, one against the foreign enemy, the other against prejudice at home."

Even Robinson could not have realized how high the personal stakes were when he refused to move to the back of the bus in 1944. Had he been convicted of the more serious charges and, as he feared, dishonorably discharged, it is doubtful that Branch Rickey, general manager of the Brooklyn National League Club, would have chosen him to integrate organized baseball in 1946. In the climate of postwar America, a black man banished from the Army could have found little popular support. It is not unreasonable to suppose that Robinson, who was already twenty-eight years old when he joined the Brooklyn Dodgers, might never have made it to the major leagues had he been forced to wait for another man to act as trailblazer. Fortunately, his defiance had precisely the opposite effect. His Army experiences, which graphically illustrated the black man's lot in America, also demonstrated Jackie Robinson's courage and pride. These were the very qualities that would prove essential in making the assault on baseball's color line.

THREE

Jackie Robinson's Signing:
The Untold Story

With John Thorn

It was the first week of October 1945. In the Midwest the Detroit Tigers and Chicago Cubs faced off in the final World Series of the World War II era. Two thousand miles away photographer Maurice Terrell arrived at an almost deserted Lane Field, the home of the minor league San Diego Padres. Terrell's assignment was as secretive as some wartime operations: to surreptitiously photograph three black baseball players wearing the uniforms of the Kansas City Royals, a Negro League all-star team. Within three weeks one of these players would rank among the most celebrated and intriguing figures in the nation. But in early October 1945, as he worked out with his teammates in the empty stadium, Jackie Robinson represented the best-kept secret in sports history.

Terrell shot hundreds of motion-picture frames of Robinson and his cohorts. A few appeared in print but the existence of the additional images remained unknown for four decades, until unearthed in 1987 at the Baseball Hall of Fame by John Thorn. This discovery triggered an investigation that has led to startling revelations regarding Brooklyn Dodger president Branch Rickey's original plan to shatter baseball's long-standing color line; the relationship between these two historic figures; and the still controversial issue of black managers in baseball.

The popularly held "frontier" image of Jackie Robinson as a lone gunman facing down a hostile mob has always dominated the integration saga. But new information related to the Terrell photos reveals that while Robinson was the linchpin to Branch Rickey's strategy, *in October 1945 Rickey intended to announce the signing of not just Jackie Robinson, but several stars from the Negro Leagues at once.* Political pressures, however, forced Rickey's hand, thrusting Robinson alone into a spotlight that he never relinquished.

The path to these revelations began with Thorn's discovery of the Terrell photographs in a collection donated to the Baseball Hall of Fame by *Look* magazine in 1954. The images depict a youthful, muscular Robinson in a battered hat and baggy uniform fielding from his position at shortstop, batting with a black catcher crouched behind him, trapping a third black player in a rundown between third and home, and sprinting along the base paths more like a former track star than a baseball player. A woman with her back to the action is the only figure visible in the vacant stands. The contact sheets bore the imprinted date October 7, 1945.

The images perplexed Thorn. He knew that the momentous announcement of Jackie Robinson's signing with the Montreal Royals had not occurred until October 23, 1945. Before that date his recruitment by Rickey had been a tightly guarded secret. Why, then, had a *Look* photographer taken such an interest in Robinson two weeks earlier? Where had the pictures been taken? And why was Robinson already wearing a Royals uniform?

Thorn called Jules Tygiel, the author of *Baseball's Great Experiment: Jackie Robinson and His Legacy*, to see if he could shed some light on the photos. Tygiel had no knowledge of them, but he did have in his files a 1945 manuscript by newsman Arthur Mann, who frequently wrote for *Look*. The article, drafted with Rickey's cooperation, had been intended to announce the Robinson signing but had never been published. The pictures, they concluded, had doubtless been shot to accompany Mann's article, and they decided to find out the story behind the photo session. Tygiel set out to trace Robinson's activities in early October 1945. Thorn headed for the Library of Congress to examine Branch Rickey's personal papers, including his correspondence and business records, which had been unavailable at the time Tygiel wrote his book.

The clandestine nature of the photo session did not surprise the researchers. From the moment he had arrived in Brooklyn in 1942, determined to end baseball's Jim Crow traditions, Rickey had feared that premature disclosure of his intentions might doom his bold design. Rickey therefore moved slowly and deliberately during his first three years in Brooklyn. He informed the Dodger owners of his plans but took few others into his confidence. He began to explore the issue and devised elaborate strategies to cover up his attempts to scout black players.

In the spring of 1945, as Rickey prepared to accelerate his scouting efforts, integration advocates, emboldened by the impending end of World War II, escalated their campaign to desegregate baseball.

Amidst this heated atmosphere, Rickey created an elaborate smokescreen to obscure his scouting of black players. In May 1945 he announced the formation of a new franchise, the Brooklyn Brown Dodgers, and a new Negro League, the United States League. Rickey then dispatched his best talent hunters to observe black ballplayers, ostensibly for the Brown Dodgers but in reality for the Brooklyn National League club.

A handwritten memorandum in the Rickey papers offers a rare glimpse at Rickey's emphasis on secrecy in his instructions to Dodger scouts. The document, signed by Charles D. Clark and accompanied by a Negro National League schedule for April–May 1945, is headlined "Job Analysis," and defines the following "Duties: under supervision of management of club:

1. To establish contact (silent) with all clubs (local or general).
2. To gain knowledge and abilities of all players.
3. To report all possible material (players).
4. Prepare weekly reports of activities.
5. Keep composite report of outstanding players. . . . To travel and cover player whenever management so desire."

Clark's "Approach" [sic] was to "Visit game and loose [sic] self in stands; Keep statistical report (speed, power, agility, ability, fielding, batting, etc.) by score card"; and "Leave immediately after game."

Curiously, Clark listed his first "Objective" as being "to cover Negro teams for possible major league talent." Yet according to his later accounts, Rickey had told most Dodger scouts that they were evaluating talent for a new Brown Dodger franchise. Had Rickey confided in Clark, a figure so obscure as to escape prior mention in the voluminous Robinson literature? Dodger superscout and Rickey confidante Clyde Sukeforth has no recollection of Clark, raising the possibility that Clark was not part of the Dodger family, but perhaps someone connected with black baseball. Had Clark himself interpreted his instructions in this manner?

Whatever the answer, Rickey successfully diverted attention from his true motives. Nonetheless, mounting interest in the integration issue threatened Rickey's careful planning. In the summer of 1945 Rickey constructed yet another facade. The Dodger president took Dan Dodson, a New York University sociologist who chaired Mayor Fiorello LaGuardia's Committee on Unity, into his confidence and requested that Dodson form a Committee on Baseball ostensibly to study the possibility of integration. In reality, the committee would provide the illusion of action while Rickey quietly completed his own preparations to sign several black players at once. "This was one of the toughest decisions I ever had to make while in office," Dodson later confessed. "The major purpose I could see for the committee was that it was a stall for time. . . . Yet had Mr. Rickey not delivered . . . I would have been totally discredited."

Thus by late August, even as Rickey's extensive scouting reports had led him to focus in on Jackie Robinson as his standard bearer, few people in or out of the Dodger organization suspected that a breakthrough was imminent. On August 28 Rickey and Robinson held their historic meeting at the Dodgers' Montague Street offices in downtown Brooklyn. Robinson signed an agreement to accept a contract with the Montreal Royals, the top Dodger affiliate, by November 1. Rickey, still concerned with secrecy, impressed upon Robinson the need to maintain silence until further preparations had been made. Robinson could tell the momentous news to his family and fianceè, but no one else.

For the conspiratorial Rickey, further subterfuge was necessary to keep the news sheltered while continuing the arrangements. Rumors about Robinson's visit had already spread through the world of black baseball. To stifle speculation Rickey "leaked" an adulterated version of the incident to black sportswriter Wendell Smith. Smith, who had recommended Robinson to Rickey and advised Rickey on the integration project, doubtless knew the true story behind the meeting. On September 8, however, he reported in the *Pittsburgh Courier* that the "sensational shortstop" and "colorful major league dynamo" had met behind "closed doors."

"The nature of the conferences has not been revealed," wrote Smith. "It seems to be shrouded in mystery and Robinson has not made a statement since he left Brooklyn." Rickey claimed that he and Robinson had assessed "the organization of Negro baseball," but did not discuss "the possibility of Robinson becoming a member of the Brooklyn Dodgers organization."

Smith hinted broadly of future developments, noting that "It does not seem logical [Rickey] should call in a rookie player to discuss the future organization of Negro baseball." He closed with the tantalizing thought that "it appears that the Brooklyn boss has a plan on his mind that extends further than just the future of Negro baseball as an organization." But the subterfuge succeeded. Neither black nor white reporters pursued the issue further.

Rickey, always sensitive to criticism by New York sports reporters and understanding the historic significance of his actions, wanted to be sure that his version of the integration breakthrough and his role in it be accurately portrayed. To guarantee this he expanded his circle of conspirators to include freelance writer Arthur Mann. In the weeks following the Robinson meeting, Mann, Rickey's close friend and later a Dodger employee, authored at the Mahatma's behest a three-thousand-word manuscript to be published simultaneously with the announcement of the signing.

Although it is impossible to confirm this, it seems highly likely that Maurice Terrell's photos, commissioned by *Look*, were destined to accompany Mann's article. Clearer prints of the negatives revealed to Thorn and Tygiel that Terrell had taken the pictures in San Diego's Lane Stadium. This fits in with Robinson's fall itinerary. In the aftermath of his meeting with Rickey, Robinson had returned briefly to the Kansas City Monarchs. With the Dodger offer securing his future and the relentless bus trips of the Negro League schedule wearing him down, he had left the Monarchs before season's end and returned home to Pasadena, California. In late September he hooked up with Chet Brewer's Kansas City Royals, a postseason barnstorming team that toured the Pacific Coast, competing against other Negro League teams and major and minor league all-star squads. Thus the word "Royals" on Robinson's uniform, which had so piqued the interest of Thorn and Tygiel, ironically turned out not to relate to Robinson's future team in Montreal, but rather to his interim employment in California.

For further information Tygiel contacted Chet Brewer, who at age eighty still lived in Los Angeles. Brewer, one of the great pitchers of the Jim Crow era, had known Robinson well. He had followed Robinson's spectacular athletic career at UCLA and in 1945 they became teammates on the Monarchs. "Jackie was major league all the way," recalls Brewer. "He had the fastest reflexes I ever saw in a player." With Brewer's Royals, Robinson was always the first in the clubhouse and the first one on the field. "Satchel Paige was just the opposite," laughs Brewer. "He would get there just as the game was about to start and come running on the field still tying his shoe."

Robinson particularly relished facing major league all-star squads. Against Bob Feller, Robinson slashed two doubles. "Jack was running crazy on the bases," a Royal teammate remembers. In one game he upended shortstop Gerry Priddy of the Washington Senators. Priddy angrily complained about the hard slide in an exhibition game. "Any time I put on a uniform," retorted Robinson, "I play to win." The fire in his playing notwithstanding, Robinson maintained his pledge to Rickey. Neither Brewer nor any of his teammates suspected the secret that Robinson faithfully kept inside him.

Brewer recalls that Robinson and two other Royals journeyed from Los Angeles to San Diego on a day when the team was not scheduled to play. He identified the catcher in the photos as Buster Haywood and the other player as Royals third baseman Herb Souell. Souell is no longer living, but Haywood, who, like Brewer resides in Los Angeles, has vague recollections of the event, which he incorrectly remembers as occurring in Pasadena.

Robinson had befriended Haywood the preceding year while coaching basketball in Texas. He recruited the catcher and Souell, his former Monarch teammate, to "work out" with him. All three wore their Royal uniforms. Haywood found neither Robinson's request nor the circumstances unusual. Although he was unaware that they were being photographed, Haywood still can describe the session accurately. "We didn't know what was going on," he states. "We'd hit and throw and run from third base to home plate."

The San Diego pictures provide a rare glimpse of the pre-Montreal Robinson. The article that they were to accompany and related correspondence in the Library of Congress offers even rarer insights into Rickey's thinking. The unpublished Mann manuscript was entitled "The Negro and Baseball: The National Game Faces a Racial Challenge Long Ignored." As Mann doubtless based his account on conversations with Rickey, and since Rickey's handwritten comments appear in the margin, it stands as the earliest "official" account of the Rickey-Robinson story and reveals many of the concerns confronting Rickey in September 1945.

One of the most striking features of the article is the language used to refer to Robinson. Mann, reflecting the blind racism typical of postwar America, insensitively portrays Robinson as the "first Negro chattel in the so-called National pastime." At another point he writes, "Rickey felt the boy's sincerity," appropriate language perhaps for an eighteen-year-old prospect, but not for a twenty-six-year-old former army officer.

"The Negro and Baseball" consists largely of the now familiar Rickey-Robinson story. Mann recreated Rickey's haunting 1904 experience as collegiate coach of black baseball player Charlie Thomas, who, when denied access to a hotel, cried and rubbed his hands, chanting, "Black skin! Black skin! If I could only make 'em white." Mann described the search for the "right" man, the formation of the United States League as a cover for scouting operations, the reasons for selecting Robinson, and the fateful drama of the initial Rickey-Robinson confrontation.

Other sections, however, graphically illustrate which issues Rickey deemed significant. Mann repeatedly cites the financial costs incurred by the Dodgers: $5,000 to scout Cuba, $6,000 to scout Mexico, $5,000 to establish the Brooklyn Brown Dodgers. The final total reaches $25,000, a modest sum considering the ultimate returns, but one that Rickey felt would counter his skinflint image.

Rickey's desire to dispel the notion that political pressures had motivated his actions also emerges clearly. Mann had suggested that upon arriving in Brooklyn in 1942, Rickey "was besieged by telephone calls, telegrams, and letters of petition in behalf of black ballplayers," and that this "staggering pile of missives were so inspired to convince him that he and the Dodgers had been selected as a kind of guinea pig." In his marginal comments, Rickey vehemently objected to this notion. "No!" he wrote in a strong dark script, "I began all this as soon as I went to Brooklyn." Explaining why he had never attacked the subject during his two decades as general manager of the St. Louis Cardinals, Rickey referred to the segregated conditions in that city. "St. Louis never permitted Negro patrons in the grandstand," he wrote, describing a policy he had apparently felt powerless to change.

Mann also devoted two of his twelve pages to a spirited attack on the Negro Leagues. He repeated Rickey's charges that "They are the poorest excuse for the word league" and documented the prevalence of barnstorming, the uneven scheduling, absence of contracts, and dominance of booking agents. Mann revealingly traces Rickey's distaste for the Negro Leagues to the "outrageous" guarantees demanded by New York booking agent William Leuschner to place black teams in Ebbets Field while the Dodgers were on the road.

Rickey's misplaced obsession with the internal disorganization of the Negro Leagues had substantial factual basis. But in transforming the black circuits into major villains of Jim Crow baseball, Rickey had an ulterior motive. In his September 8 article, Wendell Smith addressed the issue of "player tampering," asking "Would [Rickey] not first approach the owner of these Negro teams who have these stars under contract?" Rickey, argued Smith in what might have been an unsuccessful preemptive strike, "is obligated to do so and his record as a businessman indicated that he would." As Smith may have known, Rickey maintained that Negro League players did not sign valid contracts and became free agents at the end of each season. The Mahatma thus had no intention of compensating Negro League teams for the players he signed. His repeated attacks on black baseball, including the Mann article, served to justify this questionable practice.

The one respect in which "The Negro and Baseball" departs radically from common perceptions of the Robinson legend is in its depiction of Robinson as one of a group of blacks about to be signed by the Dodgers. Mann's manuscript reveals that Rickey did not intend for Robinson, usually viewed as a solitary standard bearer, to withstand the pressures alone. "Determined not to be charged with merely nibbling at the problem," wrote Mann, "Rickey went all out and brought in two more Negro players," and "consigned them, with Robinson, to the Dodgers' top farm club, the Montreal Royals." Mann named pitcher Don Newcombe and, surprisingly, outfielder Sam Jethroe as Robinson's future teammates.

As Mann's report indicates, and subsequent correspondence from Rickey confirms, *Rickey did not plan to announce the signing of just one black player.* Whether the recruitment of additional blacks had always been his intention or whether he had reached his decision after meeting with Robinson in August is unclear. But by late September, when he provided information to Mann for his article, Rickey had clearly decided to bring in other Negro League stars.

During the first weekend in October, Dodger coach Chuck Dressen fielded a major league all-star team in a series of exhibition games against Negro League standouts at Ebbets Field. Rickey took the opportunity to interview at least three black pitching prospects, Newcombe, Roy Partlow and John Wright. The following week he met with catcher Roy Campanella. Campanella and Newcombe, at least, believed they had been approached to play for the Brown Dodgers.

At the same time, Rickey decided to postpone publication of Mann's manuscript. In a remarkable letter sent from the World Series in Chicago on October 7, Rickey informed Mann:

> We just can't go now with the article. The thing isn't dead,—not at all. It is more alive than ever and that is the reason we can't go with any publicity at this time. There is more involved in the situation than I had contemplated. Other players are in it and it may be that I can't clear these players until after the December meetings, possibly not until after the first of the year. You must simply sit in the boat. . . . There is a November 1 deadline on Robinson,—you know that. I am undertaking to extend that date until January 1st so as to give me time to sign plenty of players and make one break on the complete story. Also, quite obviously it might not be good to sign Robinson with other and possibly better players unsigned.

The revelations and tone of this letter surprise Robinson's widow, Rachel, forty years after the event. Rickey "was such a deliberate man," she recalls, "and this letter is so urgent. He must have been very nervous as he neared his goal. Maybe he was nervous that the owners would turn him down and having five people at the door instead of just one would have been more powerful."

Events in the weeks after October 7 justified Rickey's nervousness and forced him to deviate from the course stated in the Mann letter. Candidates in New York City's upcoming November elections, most notably black Communist City Councilman Ben Davis, made baseball integration a major plank in the campaign.

Mayor LaGuardia's liberal supporters also sought to exploit the issue.

Professor Dodson's Committee on Baseball had prepared a report outlining a modest, long-range strategy for bringing blacks into the game and described the New York teams, because of the favorable political and racial climate in the city, as in a "choice position to undertake this pattern of integration." LaGuardia wanted Rickey's permission to make a preelection announcement that "baseball would shortly begin signing Negro players," as a result of the committee's work.

Rickey, a committee member, had long ago subverted the panel to his own purposes. By mid-October, however, the committee had become "an election football." Again unwilling to risk the appearance of succumbing to political pressure and thereby surrendering what he viewed as his rightful role in history, Rickey asked LaGuardia to delay his comments. Rickey hurriedly contacted Robinson, who had joined a barnstorming team in New York en route to play winter ball in Venezuela, and dispatched him to Montreal. On October 23, 1945, with Rickey's carefully laid plans scuttled, the Montreal Royals announced the signing of Robinson, and Robinson alone.

The premature revelation of Rickey's racial breakthrough had important ramifications for the progress of baseball's "great experiment." Mann's article never appeared. *Look*, having lost its exclusive, published two strips of the Terrell pictures in its November 27, 1945 issue accompanying a brief summary of the Robinson story. The unprocessed film negatives and contact sheets were loaded into a box and nine years later shipped to the National Baseball Hall of Fame, where they remained, along with a picture of Jethroe, unpacked until April 1987.

Newcombe, Campanella, Wright, and Partlow all joined the Dodger organization the following spring. Jethroe became a victim of the "deliberate speed" of baseball integration. Rickey did not interview Jethroe in 1945. Since few teams followed the Dodger lead, the fleet, powerful outfielder remained in the Negro Leagues until 1948, when Rickey finally bought his contract from the Cleveland Buckeyes for $5,000. Jethroe had two spectacular seasons at Montreal before Rickey, fearing a "surfeit of colored boys on the Brooklyn club," profitably sold him to the Boston Braves for $100,000. Jethroe won the Rookie of the Year Award in 1950, but his delayed entry into organized baseball foreshortened what should have been a stellar career. To this day, Jethroe remains unaware of how close he came to joining Robinson, Newcombe, and Campanella in the pantheon of integration pioneers.

Beyond these revelations about the Robinson signing, the Library of

Congress documents add surprisingly little to the familiar contours of the integration saga. The Rickey papers copiously detail his post-Dodger career as general manager of the Pittsburgh Pirates but are strangely silent about the critical 1944–48 period. Records for these years probably remained with the Dodger organization, which claims to have no knowledge of their whereabouts. National League documents for these years remain closed to the public.

There is one letter of interest from Rickey to Robinson, in which the old man offers some encouragement to Jackie's budding managerial ambitions. In 1950, following his fourth season with the Dodgers, Jackie Robinson wrote to Branch Rickey about the possibility of employment in baseball when his playing days had ended—especially, about managing. Robinson's original letter cannot be found in either the Rickey papers or the Robinson family archives. However, Rickey's reply, dated December 31, 1950, survives.

Rickey had recently left the Dodgers after an unsuccessful struggle to wrest control of the team from Walter O'Malley. He responded to Robinson's inquiry with a long and equivocal answer.

On the subject of managing, Rickey replied optimistically, "I hope that the day will soon come when it will be entirely possible, as it is entirely right, that you can be considered for administrative work in baseball, particularly in the direction of field management." Rickey claimed to have told several writers that "I do not know of any player in the game today who could, in my judgment, manage a major league club better than yourself," but that the news media had inexplicably ignored these comments.

Yet Rickey tempered his encouragement with remarks that seemed to dodge Robinson's request. "As I have often expressed to you," he wrote, "I think you carry a great responsibility for your people . . . and I cannot close this letter without admonishing you to prepare yourself to do a widely useful work, and, at the same time, dignified and effective in the field of public relations. A part of this preparation, and I know you are smiling, for you have already guessed my oft repeated suggestion—to finish your college course meritoriously and get your degree." This advice, according to Rachel Robinson, was a "matter of routine" between the two men since their first meeting.

Rickey concluded with the promise, which seems to hinge on the completion of a college degree, that "it would be a great pleasure for me to be your agent in placing you in a big job after your playing days are finished."

Shortly after writing this letter Rickey became the general manager of the

Pittsburgh Pirates. Had Robinson ended his playing career before Rickey left the Pirates, perhaps the Mahatma would have made good on his pledge. But Rickey resigned from the Pirates following the 1955 season, one year before Robinson's retirement.

Robinson's 1950 letter to Rickey marked only the beginning of his quest to see a black pilot in the major leagues. In 1951 he hoped to gain experience by managing in the Puerto Rican winter league, but, according to the *New York Post*, commissioner Happy Chandler withheld his approval, forcing Robinson to cancel his plans. On November 30, 1952, the Dodgers' star raised the prospect of a black manager in a televised interview on *Youth Wants to Know*, stating that both he and Roy Campanella had been "approached" on the subject. In 1953, after the Dodgers had fired manager Chuck Dressen, speculation arose that either Robinson or Pee Wee Reese might be named to the post. But the team bypassed both men and selected veteran minor league manager Walter Alston.

Upon his retirement in 1956, Robinson, who had begun to manifest signs of the diabetes that would plague the rest of his life, had lost much of his enthusiasm for managing, but nonetheless would probably have accepted yet another pioneering role. "He had wearied of the travel," states Rachel Robinson, "and no longer wanted to manage. He just wanted to be asked as a recognition of his accomplishments, his abilities as a strategist and to show that white men could be led by a black."

In any case, Robinson's greatest pioneering work came as a player. Though Rickey apparently intended that Jackie be just one of a number of black players signed at one time, the scuttling of those plans laid the success or failure of the assault on Jim Crow disproportionately on the capable shoulders of Jackie Robinson, who had always occupied center stage in Rickey's thinking. While this greatly intensified the pressures on the man, it also enhanced his legend immensely. Firmly fixed in the public mind as the sole pathfinder, rather than group leader, he became the lightning rod for supporter and opponent alike, attracting the responsibility, the opprobrium, and ultimately the acclaim for his historic achievement.

FOUR

Afterword to *Baseball's Great Experiment*

As historian Steve Riess has commented, the Jackie Robinson story is to Americans what the Passover story is to Jews: it must be told to every generation so that we never forget. But if this is true, and it most assuredly is, what is it that we must not forget? The subtitle for *Baseball's Great Experiment* was *Jackie Robinson and His Legacy.* What, however, is the legacy of Jackie Robinson fifty years after his triumph, in an America in which the Voting Rights Act, school busing, affirmative action, and other integration strategies find themselves increasingly on the defensive; an America in which black nationalism and separatism, the antithesis of Robinson's vision, win a welcome audience in African-American communities; an America in which the tenets of *Brown v. the Board of Education*, the cornerstone judicial ruling of the civil rights era, are challenged by the sole African-American Supreme Court justice?

Ironically, amidst this growing retreat from integrationist values, Jackie Robinson has become, if possible, even more of a national icon, more firmly embedded in American culture than ever before. His name itself has long since entered our language as a synonym for the first to enter a field, the pathbreaker, the pioneer. At least three statues of Robinson have appeared: in Los Angeles, in Daytona Beach, Florida, and in Montreal, where a sculpted Robinson holds the hands of two children, one black and one white. Public schools, like the Jackie Robinson Academy in Long Beach, California, and the Jackie Robinson Junior High School in Brooklyn, bear his name. The Library of Congress lists fifteen books published about Jackie Robinson since 1983, thirteen of them addressed to juvenile and young adult readers.[1] Indeed, he has become a staple of social studies courses, usually segregated, ironically, into the annual celebration of African-American history month. There have been two television movies (including *The Court-Martial of Jackie Robinson*, in which Joe Louis and Dodger scout

Clyde Sukeforth improbably wait outside a 1944 Texas military hearing room for the fateful verdict), a murder mystery (*The Plot to Kill Jackie Robinson*),[2] a mercifully short-lived Broadway musical entitled *The First*, and at least two itinerant one-man shows devoted to his life.

Just as each generation has retold the Jackie Robinson story, each has reinterpreted his character and contributions. From the start, Robinson has always assumed not just heroic but biblical proportions. In the 1940s and 1950s, many in both the black and white communities saw Robinson as a Moses, leading his people out of the wilderness to the promised land. In the years before Martin Luther King, Jr., Robinson, more than any other individual, personified the era's liberal optimism and reaffirmed the possibility of racial integration.

Historian Lerone Bennett has commented, "Integration has never been tried in this country. It has not even been defined."[3] But for millions of Americans the experiment launched by Branch Rickey and Jackie Robinson not only defined integration but created an allegory for the nation's future. Their bold enterprise rested on several fundamental, and soon to be widely shared, assumptions: discrimination, not racial inferiority, blocked African-American advancement; the removal of discriminatory barriers would allow blacks to demonstrate their talents and prove their worth; white participants and observers, although initially resistant, would, in the words of Alexander Pope, often quoted by Branch Rickey, "first endure," but "then embrace" first the standard-bearer and then the concept of integration; success would inspire (and indeed necessitate) emulation among rivals and embolden other African Americans to challenge racial strictures. These Joshuas, accepting the mantle of leadership from Robinson's Moses, would bring the walls of Jim Crow tumbling down. Rickey and Robinson consciously crafted this parable; Robinson's charismatic dynamism infused it with substance. At least in its early stages, the Robinson saga offered a blueprint for liberal dreams of racial equality in post–World War II America.

Conservatives as well as liberals could embrace this allegory. This drama, after all, had been enacted by a pair of men usually identified as Republicans. Rickey, throughout his life, endorsed conservative causes.[4] Robinson endeared himself to Republicans by his ill-conceived 1949 denunciation of Paul Robeson and support for Richard Nixon in 1960. Even in Robinson's more characteristically moderate political mode, he maintained a Republican affiliation and advocated the virtues of American capitalism. More significantly, the integration of the Brooklyn Dodgers embodied several traditional conservative themes: individual achievement, meritocracy, and progress without government interference. As late as 1950, Rickey (who would later support civil rights laws) wrote, "As I see it, legislative force can delay rather than accelerate the solution" to the nation's racial problems.[5] The Robinson saga thus united people across a broad political spectrum. What other American fable could elicit encomiums over one four-day period, as Robinson's did in 1987, from George Will, William Safire, and the Communist *Daily Worker*?[6]

Robinson's triumph had a profound effect on African Americans, further cementing the dominance of integrationist values. Black nationalist and separatist visions had proliferated in the 1920s with Marcus Garvey and others and would resurface in the 1960s with Malcolm X. But these philosophies reached a nadir in public support in the post–World War II years.[7] Integrationist thought reigned virtually unopposed in black America in the 1940s and 1950s.

The strange career of Negro League historiography illustrates this phenomenon. In the 1960s most Americans had forgotten that the Negro Leagues had ever existed. As late as 1982, the essential Negro League library consisted of a handful of titles.[8] Recent years, however, have witnessed an unprecedented celebration of baseball in the Jim Crow era. Dozens of books, including general overviews, oral histories, encyclopedias, photo books, several excellent team histories, numerous biographies and autobiographies, reprints of long-out-of-print classics like Sol White's 1906 *History of Colored Baseball*, and many volumes devoted to a juvenile and young adult audience, have appeared.[9] Both the Macmillan *Baseball Encyclopedia* and *Total Baseball* now include Negro League sections. Several documentaries, including Ken Burns's *Baseball*, have described black baseball. August Wilson's Pulitzer Prize–winning play, *Fences*, employed the frustration of the Negro League star as its central motif. Major League teams host Negro League reunions, and former players are featured guests at card shows and autograph sessions. The sale of Negro League uniform replicas has become a flourishing business. In short, Jim Crow baseball has at long last been integrated into the American cultural mainstream.

The new Negro League history reminds us of the vitality of black baseball before Jackie Robinson and the dual tragedy often noted by Sam Lacy. "I felt that not only were blacks deprived of the opportunity to make some money," laments the great African-American sportswriter, "but that whites were being deprived of the opportunity to see these fellows perform. . . . Both were being cheated."[10]

But a revisionist streak that stands the traditional Robinson saga on its head runs through many of these accounts. In this version, Rickey and Robinson emerge as the villains who destroyed the Negro Leagues.[11] Rickey,

motivated neither by idealism nor a desire to win pennants, selfishly sought
to prevent Negro League teams from attracting potential Brooklyn Dodgers
fans. When his attempts to become the czar of an all-black United States
League failed, according to one variation, he cut his losses by signing some
of the players he had scouted. Even those who accept the United States
League as a smokescreen see Rickey's primary goal as capturing the Negro
League market. Rickey compounded this strategy by raiding the black teams
and refusing to pay, or underpaying, Negro League owners for rights to
their players. Robinson receives credit for his courage and pathbreaking
role but, because of his unflinching support of Rickey's strategies and his
own pointed criticisms of the Negro Leagues, is cast as an ingrate to the
institution which had kept baseball alive in black America.

Many of these studies take their lead from playwright Amiri Baraka, who
recalled the Negro Leagues as "extensions of all of us, there, in a way that
the Yankees and Dodgers and what not could never be . . . the collective
black aura that only can be duplicated with black conversation or music."[12]
Sociologist Harry Edwards, questioning the process that Rickey employed,
notes the great paradox of baseball integration: that by destroying the Negro
Leagues, integration limited, rather than expanded, opportunities for blacks
in baseball. Since organized baseball initially culled only the top African-
American stars and for decades failed to hire blacks as managers, coaches,
and scouts, far fewer blacks earned their living from baseball after 1950
than at any previous time in the twentieth century. Edwards argues that an
alternative plan for integration that incorporated the Negro Leagues into
organized baseball might better have served black America.[13]

A 1996 conference presentation asked: "Could the Negro Leagues Have
Been Saved?"[14] But what is significant is how seldom this question, or its
corollary, "Should the Negro Leagues be saved?" was asked during the 1940s
and 1950s. What distinguishes Baraka's paean to the spirit of the Negro
Leagues is its rarity. While Baraka and others have crafted a nostalgia for
black baseball, few in the 1940s posited it as a preferable alternative to
major league integration. Edwards's proposition for prolonging the Negro
Leagues, even in the unlikely event that it would have been feasible, is
strikingly similar to that of obstructionist New York Yankee owner Larry
MacPhail in 1946, who offered a similar suggestion as a means to forestall
desegregation. MacPhail's solution was universally criticized by black and
white advocates of equality.

The baseball model, fears Edwards, implied that "overall Black integration into the mainstream of American life [would] necessarily demand the
denigration, abandonment, and ultimate collapse of parallel Black institu-

tions."[15] But unlike other African-American entities such as black churches, music, and colleges that survived and flourished after the civil rights years, the Negro Leagues lacked any legitimacy outside of a segregationist context. Robinson's critique of the Negro Leagues stemmed not from any personal hostility to African-American culture but from his perception of these teams as Jim Crow institutions. Most African Americans agreed. What killed the Negro Leagues was not Rickey's calculated callousness, nor Robinson's ingratitude, but the clearly stated preference of black fans for even the barest rudiments of an interracial alternative.

Thus, in the 1950s and early 1960s, integration became the only game in town. As professional and major college sports increasingly became dominated by African-American athletes and as the civil rights movement scored victory after victory in the courts, in the streets, and ultimately in the Congress, Americans celebrated Jackie Robinson as the prophet of these advances. A closer look at the racial realities of baseball, however, foretold the difficulties awaiting the broader society. Given the spectacular success of the first black players to reach the majors, desegregation of most clubs advanced with remarkable hesitancy. Many teams adopted a de facto quota system limiting black access and disproportionately relegating blacks to specific positions. While superstar African-American athletes experienced minimal difficulty reaching the major leagues, those of average and even above average talent often lost out to less-talented whites. Racism and discrimination plagued black players in spring training, off-field accommodations, fan reactions, salaries, and endorsement opportunities. Most tellingly, major league organizations made no efforts, and apparently gave minimal thought, to bring blacks into coaching, managing, front office, or ownership roles. Robinson's repeated critiques of these conditions won him further praise from some but a growing enmity and disdain from others. In a society experimenting with new visions of race relations, Robinson, and sports in general, continued to symbolize the possibilities, rather than the limitations, of integration.

In the 1960s, Robinson remained a heroic figure to the majority of Americans, both black and white. To a new generation of black nationalists and other 1960s radicals, however, he increasingly assumed the garb of a false prophet. In November 1963 Malcolm X savagely attacked Robinson in an "Open Letter" in the *Amsterdam News*, as the creation of a succession of "White Boss(es)," for whom he was "still trying to win 'The Big Game.'" Robinson, alleged Malcolm, had "never shown appreciation for the support given [him] by the Negro masses." Robinson had misled African Americans in the Robeson incident, the Nixon campaign, and now his alliance with Nelson Rockefeller. "Just who are you playing ball for today, good Friend?" taunted Malcolm.[16] Amiri Baraka would later deride Robinson as a "synthetic colored guy" who was "imperfected" at the "California laboratories of USC" whose "ersatz 'blackness' could represent the shadow of the Negro integrating into America."[17]

It is not surprising that Robinson would become a target of radicals in the 1960s. The assault on Robinson by black nationalists reflected not merely his perceived political misdeeds or shift to the right but two fundamentally different world views. Robinson had committed his life to a heartfelt belief in the malleability of United States society and the potential inclusiveness of the American Dream. Malcolm X and others during the sixties had jettisoned these visions and rummaged through a stockpile of competing ideologies for alternatives.

Ironically, militant critics ignored how central Robinson had made the message of black pride and identification to his mystique. There was nothing "ersatz" about Jackie Robinson; he was the genuine article. He had been molded not at the "laboratories of USC" but on the mean streets of Pasadena, the uneven playing fields of UCLA, and the Jim Crow buses of the United States Army. At the core of Robinson's strength and image lay his ability to compromise and accommodate without losing his essential dignity and identity. Indeed, it was Robinson's unrelenting insistence on asserting his blackness that had elevated his athletic triumph into a societal emblem.

To Robinson, integration always embodied equal participation in, rather than total submission to, American culture. In the heady integrationist atmosphere of the 1950s, Jackie and Rachel Robinson opted to reside in the white suburbs of Connecticut. But Jackie's primary energies and commitment always revolved around black America. Robinson countered the political goals of black separatism with a vision of black capitalism, in which African-American investors, helped by sympathetic whites and government assistance, would create black-owned businesses, employ black workers, generate demand among the black masses, and raise the general level of prosperity, education, and opportunity among the nation's black population. Unlike Marcus Garvey or Elijah Muhammed, who also advocated black enterprise, Robinson overoptimistically envisioned these undertakings as a wedge into full and equal participation in American society, rather than as the basis for a separate economy.[18] And, unlike some contemporary African-American conservatives, Robinson never lost sight of the need for government assistance to overcome the legacy of past discrimination to achieve these ends.

In the early 1970s Robinson assumed yet another biblical persona: that of Job, upon whom untold sufferings had descended to test his faith. His firstborn son had succumbed to drug addiction and then met an untimely death. Robinson's body was wracked by diabetes and heart ailments, his hair snow white, his eyesight fading. Roger Kahn, in *The Boys of Summer*, which introduced the Robinson saga to yet another generation, memorably described having to slow his own pace "so as not to walk too quickly" for the ailing Robinson.[19]

Most dishearteningly, Robinson had come to realize that this Moses had gone to the mountaintop, but that neither he nor his people would be allowed to enter the promised land. The game in which he had placed his hopes still neglected blacks for managerial positions. The movement to which he had devoted his life seemed in disarray. His onetime political ally, Richard Nixon, now sat in the White House, the beneficiary of "white backlash" and suitor of a "Southern strategy." The limitations of black capitalism had grown apparent. While a significant number of African Americans had been able to take advantage of the opportunities that Robinson, in no small measure, had helped engender, the persistence of poverty and the bleak descent of black urban communities into drugs, crime, and violence had begun, claiming his namesake child as an early victim.

"I cannot possibly believe that I have it made while so many black brothers and sisters are hungry, inadequately housed, insufficiently clothed, denied their dignity as they live in slums or barely exist on welfare," he wrote in his angry 1972 autobiography. Yet if Robinson's trials and disappointments had sorely shaken his faith, they had not broken it. Amidst his disillusionment about the progress of the "great experiment" he had started, Robinson nonetheless professed his hope "that some day the pendulum will swing back to the time when America seemed ready to make an effort to be a united state."[20]

His death in 1972, at age fifty-three, completed the biblical cycle. To many, Robinson's youthful sacrifices, his role as standard-bearer, and his unnatural pact with Rickey to withhold retribution had precipitated his physical decline and caused his premature passing. Jackie Robinson, they said, had died for our sins. Upon his death, Robinson ascended to the heaven reserved for the saints of American folklore. His faults and mistakes would be forgotten, his accomplishments repeatedly celebrated and romanticized. Even better, those who chose to honor him need no longer contend with his insistent voice reminding them that they had denied him his full testament, as did major league baseball at the 1972 World Series. Or so they thought.

On Opening Day 1987, major league baseball planned a fortieth-anniversary commemoration of Robinson's historic debut. Ceremonies would be held at each stadium to remind a new generation of his struggles and triumphs. Robinson's number, 42, would adorn the second-base bag prior to all games. But baseball learned, yet again, that the legacy of Jackie Robinson remained a double-edged sword. On the evening before the festivities, Los Angeles Dodger vice-president Al Campanis appeared on ABC's *Nightline* with Ted Koppel. Campanis had played shortstop alongside Robinson with the Montreal Royals in 1946 and now guided the team that had integrated the game. Yet when Koppel asked him, "Why is it that there are no black managers, no black general managers, no black owners?" Campanis responded, "I truly believe that they may not have the necessities to be, let's say, a field manager, or perhaps a general manager." When Koppel proffered Campanis "another chance to dig yourself out," the old shortstop instead buried himself deeper, describing African-American musculature and questioning the desire of blacks to assume leadership positions.

The Campanis debacle laid bare baseball's hiring practices in a manner that not even Robinson himself could have achieved. Only one team had a black manager, and only one African American, Frank Robinson, had served a significant stint as a field manager. Among the top 879 administrative positions in baseball, blacks filled only seventeen; Hispanics held another fifteen. Four teams in California—the Dodgers, Giants, Athletics, and Angels—accounted for almost two-thirds of all minority hiring. Ten out of fourteen American League teams and five of twelve National League franchises had no African Americans in management positions.[21] Although few major league executives would have been so intemperate as to state the obvious as Campanis, his comments clearly reflected a widely held sentiment. Stunned by the national outcry evoked by the *Nightline* broadcast, Baseball Commissioner Peter Ueberoth vowed to remedy the situation.[22]

Nonetheless, race relations in baseball remain far from ideal. As is characteristic of most American industries, minority ownership is nonexistent. All twenty-eight chief executive officers are white. Only three blacks have served as general managers. African-American players still voice complaints about discriminatory treatment.

In addition, the spotlight on managerial positions masked an equally disturbing development: the decline of baseball as a force in the black community. Ironically, as African-American athletes came to constitute an overwhelming majority of players in college and professional football and basketball, the proportion of American-born black players in baseball's major leagues dropped from an estimated one in four in the late 1960s to only one in six in the late 1980s. The situation in the minor leagues and in college baseball, an increasingly important source of major league talent, was even worse.[23] Surveys indicated that African Americans, who had flocked to major league ballparks in the 1950s, accounted for less than 7 percent of attendance by 1987. "It is clear," wrote *New York Times* reporter Brent Staples, "that black fans, after a romance with baseball that began at the turn of the century and flourished through the early 1950s, have abandoned the national pastime."[24]

Staples blamed the hostile reception that blacks received at many ball-parks and the well-publicized patterns of hiring bias for this disaffection. Other observers noted the virtual absence of African Americans among the scouts who identified potential major leaguers. While other sports shared baseball's paltry front office and managerial hiring record, commented Staples, "in baseball, with its mystical grip on the imagination of America, this discrimination seems particularly heinous."[25] Baseball, like American society, remains haunted by the persistence of racial inequities.

Amidst these controversies, Americans continue to resurrect Jackie Robinson in a variety of often surprising symbolic forms. As the nation absorbs large numbers of other ethnic and racial groups, the Jackie Robinson model offers an inspirational example of assimilation to new groups of Americans. The modern children's classic *In the Year of the Boar and Jackie Robinson*, written by Chinese-American writer Bette Bao Lord, tells the story of Shirley Temple Wong, a Chinese immigrant girl, whose passion for Robinson and the 1947 Dodgers facilitates her entry into American life.[26] Two years after the Rodney King riots, which often pitted the Koreans of Los Angeles against the city's blacks and Hispanics, the Dodgers signed Korean pitcher Chan Ho Park. Reporter David Margolick speculated that Park, like Jackie Robinson five decades earlier, might help to heal the gaping racial wounds.[27]

More commonly, however, the Robinson saga has begun to take on an air of wistful nostalgia. In the film *Do the Right Thing*, Spike Lee's ambivalent hero, Mookie (named presumably for a lesser black New York baseball player), parades through the Brooklyn ghetto in a Jackie Robinson Brooklyn Dodger jersey. Unlike Robinson, who lived in a presumably less complicated era and for whom the "right thing" always seemed predetermined, neither Mookie, nor Lee, nor the audience can ever discern the appropriate course of action for a young black man in modern America. When television producer Gary Alan Goldberg attempted to recreate the life of a Jewish family in the 1950s in the series *Brooklyn Bridge*, Robinson was a constant presence in the cultural background of the program. Ken Burns, the preeminent

American documentary filmmaker, consciously crafted his recent *Baseball* opus around the Robinson saga. Burns's opening narrative invoked the history of the Brooklyn Dodgers as a pastiche of the nation's history, highlighted by "baseball's finest moment—when a black man wearing number forty-two trotted out to first base." In the offbeat movie *Blue in the Face*, the ghost of Jackie Robinson materializes in a Brooklyn cigar store, to reminisce about a simpler, and inferentially better, world that we have lost.

Is this, then, to be the legacy of Jackie Robinson: to evoke an idyllic, if imaginary, past, when Americans held higher hopes and greater optimism; when the racial divide seemed bridgeable and our social problems solvable? Does Jackie Robinson, the standard-bearer of mid century liberalism, still have relevance as we approach the millennium, a more conservative and chastened nation?

It is important to remember that the 1940s and the 1950s, as Edenic as they may now seem, held no such allure at the time. The problem of Jim Crow seemed unsolvable, the challenges insurmountable, and the path uncertain. White supremacy, although weakened, remained a mainstream, not a fringe, ideology. Advocates of racial division held positions of power throughout the nation. The attack against segregation, in baseball and in society, constituted an experiment in every sense of the word, and its outcome remained uncertain. Jackie Robinson and Branch Rickey, however, launched their experiment with one fundamental, and, at the time, revolutionary premise: that all Americans inhabit this nation together and that the key to our future prosperity and happiness rests in the elimination of *all* obstacles to full participation. The responsibility for achieving this goal, they demonstrated, required the initiative and sacrifice of blacks and whites alike. This vision never entailed a surrender of ethnic and cultural distinctiveness but rather a celebration of racial pride and an inspirational model for the future.

The target assaulted by Rickey and Robinson—the seemingly impregnable wall of traditional Jim Crow—has long been obliterated. African Americans are no longer, to apply Ralph Ellison's memorable metaphor, invisible men and women. The black middle class has expanded dramatically in both size and influence. African Americans hold thousands of elected offices and other public positions, many in predominantly white communities. African-American entertainers and athletes rank among our most celebrated and beloved national figures. A retired African-American general is the preferred presidential candidate of millions of Americans. These achievements reflect not merely black accomplishments but a profound transformation of racial attitudes in white America.

Nonetheless, we have been forced to acknowledge the naivete of our earlier optimism. While millions of African Americans have benefited from the dismantling of more rigid racial thought and strictures, conditions for millions of others in our inner cities have deteriorated. The economic heritage of slavery and segregation has proved enduring and, thus far, intractable. Integrationist strategies, adopted in the 1950s and now seemingly embedded in our lives, have failed to achieve many of their stated goals. Amidst a backdrop of economic contraction and dislocation, this reality has engendered disenchantment and disillusionment on all sides of the racial divide. Discrimination and hostility toward African Americans and other minority groups remain persistent and growing realities. Politicians, mistaking the outcomes of poverty for the causes of decline, find convenient scapegoats in the embattled African-American community. Within that community, voices of hatred and division often drown out those of reconciliation. Reactions to racially charged episodes like the O. J. Simpson trial reveal the vastly different worlds and perceptions of white and black Americans.

Amidst this maelstrom we must rescue Jackie Robinson from the realm of nostalgia. We remain engrossed in the great social experiment that he began. But, as with all incomplete experiments, we must periodically reassess its progress and reinvigorate its promise. We must reinforce those strategies that work, reject those that have failed, and assay new initiatives. The Jackie Robinson saga, whether in myth or reality, has always appealed to "the better angels of our nature." Today, fifty years after he first graced us with his pride, his courage, his passion, and his vision, our nation, amidst our current failures, disappointments, and dispiriting political drift, has yet to produce a more compelling prophecy of a just, interracial society than that which we envision when we invoke the memory of Jackie Robinson.

NOTES

The author wishes to thank the following people for their critiques of earlier drafts of this afterword: Luise Custer, Peter Dreier, Bill Issel, Michael Knight, Barbara Loomis, Sheldon Meyer, Mike Pincus, David Shipp, Eric Solomon, Naomi Weinstein, and Richard Zitrin.

1. While there is still no satisfactory biography of Jackie Robinson, two recent books shed further light on his life. See Maury Allen, *Jackie Robinson: A Life Remembered* (New York, 1987), and David Falkner, *Great Time Coming: The Life of Jackie Robinson from Baseball to Birmingham* (New York, 1995).

2. Donald Honig, *The Plot to Kill Jackie Robinson* (New York, 1993).

3. Bennett quoted in Studs Terkel, *Race: How Blacks and Whites Think and Feel About an American Obsession* (New York, 1992), 380.

4. On Rickey's political views, see Stephen Fox, "The Education of Branch Rickey," *Civilization* (September/October 1995), 52–57.

5. Ibid., 55.

6. See *Newsweek* (April 13, 1987); *Fort Lauderdale Sun-Sentinel*, April 14, 1987; and *People's Daily World*, April 17, 1987. For a more recent example of Robinson's appeal to conservatives, see Steve Sailer, "How Jackie Robinson Desegregated America," *National Review* (April 8, 1996), 38–41.

7. See Harvard Sitkoff, *A New Deal for Blacks* (New York, 1978), 252–53, 333–34.

8. Prior to 1983, the best available books on the Negro Leagues were Robert Peterson, *Only the Ball Was White* (Englewood Cliffs, 1970), and John Holway, *Voices from the Great Negro Baseball Leagues* (New York, 1975). William Brashler's novel, *Bingo Long and His Traveling All-Stars and Motor Kings* (New York, 1973), and his biography, *Josh Gibson: A Life in the Negro Leagues* (New York, 1978), also helped fill the vacuum.

9. The outpouring of books on the Negro Leagues is far too voluminous to list here. However, the following studies are particularly noteworthy: Donn Rogosin, *Invisible Men: Life in Baseball's Negro Leagues* (New York, 1983); Janet Bruce, *The Kansas City Monarchs: Champions of Black Baseball* (Kansas, 1985); Rob Ruck, *Sandlot Seasons* (Evanston IL, 1986); James Overmyer, *Effa Manley and the Newark Eagles* (Metuchen NJ, 1993); Neil Lanctot, *Fair Dealing and Clean Playing: The Hilldale Club and the Development of Black Professional Baseball, 1910–1932* (Jefferson NC, 1994). There are also several good reference books, including James A. Riley, *The Biographical Encyclopedia of the Negro Baseball Leagues* (New York, 1994), and Dick Clark and Larry Lester, eds., *The Negro Leagues Book* (Cleveland, 1994). Photo histories include Bruce Chadwick, *When the Game Was Black and White: The Illustrated History of the Negro Leagues* (New York, 1992), and Phil Dixon and Patrick J. Hannigan, *The Negro Baseball Leagues: A Photographic History* (Mattituck NY, 1992). There are also many biographies and autobiographies of former Negro League stars now available.

10. Ron Fimrite, "Sam Lacy: Black Crusader," *Sports Illustrated* (October 29, 1994), 91.

11. For examples, see Rogosin, 208–10; Bruce, 111; and John Holway, *Blackball Stars: Negro League Pioneers* (Westport, CT, 1988), xi–xvi.

12. Amiri Baraka, *Autobiography* (New York, 1984), 35.

13. See Edwards's review of *Baseball's Great Experiment* and *Invisible Men* in *Journal of Sport and Social Issues* (winter/spring, 1985), 41–43.

14. Lee Lowenfish, "Could the Negro Leagues Have Been Saved?" (paper

presented at the conference Breaking Baseball's Color Line: Jackie Robinson and Fifty Years of Integration, Daytona Beach, Florida, March 15, 1996).

15. Edwards, 43.

16. *New York Amsterdam News*, November 30, 1963.

17. Baraka, 35.

18. For Robinson's views, see Jackie Robinson with Alfred Duckett, *I Never Had It Made* (New York, 1972), especially chapter 17.

19. Roger Kahn, *The Boys of Summer* (New York, 1971), 402.

20. Robinson, 247, 251.

21. *USA Today*, April 9, 1987.

22. On hiring in the early 1990s, see Richard E. Lapchick, *1995 Racial Report Card* (The Center for the Study of Sport and Society, Northeastern University, 1995).

23. For figures on the 1960s, see Jack Orr, *The Black Athlete: His Story in American History* (New York, 1969), 97. For late 1980 figures, see Richard E. Lapchick and Jeffrey R. Benedict, *1994 Racial Report Card* (The Center for the Study of Sport and Society, Northeastern University, 1994). Many newspaper articles from the late 1970s through the early 1990s commented on the decline of African-American baseball players. See, for example, "Black Supply Turns from Torrent to Trickle," *Sporting News*, February 19, 1977; "Blacks not making gains; Is there a quota system?" *San Francisco Chronicle*, June 22, 1982; "College Baseball Becomes Primarily a White Game," *Los Angeles Times*, May 22, 1990; "A Scarcity of Black Division I College Players Raises Concern," *New York Times*, June 11, 1990; "Fewer Blacks Participate in Baseball," *Washington Post*, July 7, 1991; and "Blacks in Baseball," *Boston Globe*, August 4, 1991. To some extent the declining percentage of American-born blacks stemmed from the rise in Latin-American players. But even when this is taken into account, the drop in the percentage of American-born blacks between the 1960s and late 1980s was dramatic.

24. Brent Staples, "Where Are the Black Fans," *New York Times Magazine* (May 17, 1987), 28. In addition, see *New York Times*, March 23, 1986; *Boston Globe*, August 4, 1991; and "Baseball in Inner Cities: Pastime is Passed Over," *Washington Post*, July 6, 1990.

25. Staples, 28–32. On scouting, see *San Francisco Examiner*, June 24, 1982. Many people have argued that the phenomenal popularity of basketball in the black community accounts for the declining support for baseball, but it is difficult to see why this would be the case. Support for basketball has also risen in the white community, but baseball attendance among whites, at least prior to the 1994 strike, skyrocketed. There is no reason that the two cannot coexist.

26. Bette Boa Lord, *In the Year of the Boar and Jackie Robinson* (New York, 1984).

27. *New York Times*, April 10, 1994.

REFLECTIONS ON RACE AND BASEBALL

FIVE

Black Ball

The Jim Crow Years

More than fifty years have passed since what many have called the finest moment in the history of the national pastime—Jackie Robinson's shattering of the color barrier. Robinson's heroic triumph brought to an end six disgraceful decades of Jim Crow baseball. During that era some of America's greatest ballplayers plied their trade on all-black teams, in Negro Leagues, on the playing fields of Latin America, and along the barnstorming frontier of the cities and towns of the United States, but never within the major and minor league realm of "organized baseball."

Scattered evidence exists of blacks playing baseball in the antebellum period, but the first recorded black teams surfaced in Northern cities in the aftermath of the Civil War. In October 1867 the Uniques of Brooklyn hosted the Excelsiors of Philadelphia in a contest billed as the "championship of colored clubs." Before a large crowd of black and white spectators, the Excelsiors marched around the field behind a fife and drum corps before defeating the Uniques, 37–24. Two months later a second Philadelphia squad, the Pythians, dispatched a representative to the inaugural meetings of the National Association of Base Ball Players, the first organized league. The nominating committee unanimously rejected the Pythians' application, barring "any club which may be composed of one or more colored persons." Using the impeccable logic of a racist society, the committee proclaimed, "If colored clubs were admitted there would be in all probability some division of feeling, whereas, by excluding them no injury could result to anyone." The Philadelphia Pythians, however, continued their quest for interracial competition. In 1869 they became the first black team to face an all-white squad, defeating the crosstown City Items, 27–17.

In 1876 athletic entrepreneurs in the nation's metropolitan centers established the National League, which quickly came to represent the pinnacle of the sport. The new entity had no written policy regarding blacks but precluded them nonetheless through a "gentleman's agreement" among the owners. In the smaller cities and towns of America, however, where under-funded teams and fragile minor league coalitions quickly appeared and faded, individual blacks found scattered opportunities to pursue baseball careers. During the next decade at least two dozen black ballplayers sought to earn a living in this erratic professional baseball world.

Bud Fowler ranked among the best and most persistent of these trailblaz-ers. Born John Jackson in upstate New York in 1858 and raised, ironically, in Cooperstown, Fowler first achieved recognition as a twenty-year-old pitcher for a local team in Chelsea, Massachusetts. In April 1878 Fowler defeated the National League's Boston club, which included future Hall of Famers George Wright and Jim O' Rourke, 2–1 in an exhibition game, besting forty-game winner Tommy Bond. Later that season Fowler hurled three games for the Lynn Live Oaks of the International Association, the nation's first minor league, and another for Worcester in the New England League. For the next six years, he toiled for a variety of independent and semiprofessional teams in the United States and Canada. Despite a reputation as "one of the best pitchers on the continent," he failed to catch on with any major or minor league squads. In 1884, now appearing regularly as a second baseman as well as a pitcher, Fowler joined Stillwater, Minnesota, in the Northwestern League. Over the next seven seasons, Fowler played for fourteen teams in nine leagues, seldom batting less than .300 for a season. In 1886 he led the Western League in triples. "He is one of the best general players in the country," reported *Sporting Life* in 1885, "and if he had a white face he would be playing with the best of them. . . . Those who know, say there is no better second baseman in the country."

In 1886, however, a better second baseman did appear in the form of Frank Grant, perhaps the greatest black player of the nineteenth century. The light-skinned Grant, described as a "Spaniard" in the *Buffalo Express,* batted .325 for Meridien in the Eastern League. When that squad folded he joined Buffalo in the prestigious International Association and improved his average to .340, third best in the league.

Although not as talented as Fowler and Grant, bare-handed catcher Moses Fleetwood Walker achieved the highest level of play of blacks of this era. The son of an Ohio physician, Fleet Walker had studied at Oberlin College, where in 1881 he and his younger brother Welday helped launch a varsity baseball team. For the next two years, the elder Walker played for the University of Michigan and in 1883 he appeared in sixty games for the pennant-winning Toledo squad in the Northwestern League. In 1884 Toledo entered the American Association, the National League's primary rival, and Walker became the first black major leaguer. In an age when many catchers caught bare-handed and lacked chest protectors, Walker suffered frequent injuries and played little after a foul tip broke his rib in mid-July. Nonetheless, he batted .263, and pitcher Tony Mullane later called him "the best catcher I ever worked with." In July Toledo briefly signed Walker's brother Welday, who appeared in six games batting .182. The following year, Toledo dropped from the league, ending the Walkers' major league careers.

These early black players found limited acceptance among teammates, fans, and opponents. In Ontario, in 1881, Fowler's teammates forced him off the club. Walker found that Mullane and other pitchers preferred not to pitch to him. Although he acknowledged Walker's skills, Mullane confessed, "I disliked a Negro and whenever I had to pitch to him I used anything I wanted without looking at his signals." At Louisville in 1884, insults from Kentucky fans so rattled Walker that he made five errors in a game. In Richmond, after Walker had actually left the team due to injuries, the Toledo manager received a letter from "75 determined men" threatening "to mob Walker" and cause "much bloodshed" if the black catcher appeared. On August 10, 1883, Chicago White Stockings star and manager Cap Anson had threatened to cancel an exhibition game with Toledo if Walker played. The injured catcher had not been slated to start, but Toledo manager Charlie Morton defied Anson and inserted Walker into the lineup. The game proceeded without incident.

In 1887 Walker, Fowler, Grant, and five other blacks converged on the International League, a newly reorganized circuit in Canada and upstate New York, one notch below the major league level. At the same time, a new six-team entity, the League of Colored Baseball Clubs, won recognition under baseball's National Agreement, a mutual pact to honor player contracts among team owners. Thus, an air of optimism pervaded the start of the season. But 1887 would prove a fateful year for the future of blacks in baseball.

On May 6 the Colored League made its debut in Pittsburgh with "a grand street parade and a brass band concert." Twelve hundred spectators watched the hometown Keystones lose to the Gorhams of New York, 11–8. Within days, however, the new league began to flounder. The Boston franchise disbanded in Louisville on May 8, stranding its players in the Southern city. Three weeks later, league founder Walter Brown formally announced the demise of the infant circuit.

Meanwhile, in the International League, black players found their numbers growing but their status increasingly uncertain. Six of the ten teams fielded blacks, prompting *Sporting Life* to wonder, "How far will this mania for engaging colored players go?" In Newark fans marveled at the "colored battery" of Fleet Walker, dubbed the "coon catcher" by one Canadian newspaper, and "headstrong" pitcher George Stovey. Stovey, one of the greatest black pitchers of the nineteenth century, won thirty-five games, still an International League record. Frank Grant, in his second season as the Buffalo second baseman, led the league in both batting average and home runs. Bud Fowler, one of two blacks on the Binghamton squad, compiled a .350 average through early July and stole twenty-three bases.

These athletes compiled their impressive statistics under the most adverse conditions. "I could not help pitying some of the poor black fellows that played in the International League," reported a white player. "Fowler used to play second base with the lower part of his legs encased in wooden guards. He knew that about every player that came down to second base on a steal had it in for him." Both Fowler and Grant "would muff balls intentionally, so that [they] would not have to touch runners, fearing that they might injure [them]." In addition, "About half the pitchers try their best to hit these colored players when [they are] at bat." Grant, whose Buffalo teammates had refused to sit with him for a team portrait in 1886, reportedly saved himself from a "drubbing" at their hands in 1887, only by "the effective use of a club." In Toronto, fans chanted "Kill the Nigger" at Grant, and a local newspaper headline declared, "THE COLORED PLAYERS DISTASTEFUL." In late June, Bud Fowler's Binghamton teammates refused to take the field unless the club removed him from the lineup. Soon after, on July 7, the Binghamton club submitted to these demands, releasing Fowler and a black teammate, a pitcher named Renfroe.

The most dramatic confrontations between black and white players occurred on the Syracuse squad, where a clique of refugees from the Southern League exacerbated racial tensions. In spring training, the club included a catcher named Dick Male, who, rumor had it, was a light-skinned black named Richard Johnson. Male charged "that the man calling him a Negro is himself a black liar" but when released after a poor preseason performance, he returned to his old club, Zanesville, in the Ohio State League, and resumed his true identity as Richard Johnson. In May, Syracuse signed nineteen-year-old black pitcher Robert Higgins, angering the Southern clique. On May 25, Higgins appeared in his first International League game in Toronto. "THE SYRACUSE PLOTTERS," as a *Sporting News* headline called his teammates, undermined his debut. According to one account they "seemed to want the Toronto team to knock Higgins out of the box, and time and again they fielded so badly that the home team were enabled to secure many hits after the side had been retired."

"A disgusting exhibition," admonished *The Toronto World*. "They succeeded in running Male out of the club," reported a Newark paper, "and they will do the same with Higgins." One week later two Syracuse players refused to pose for a team picture with Higgins. When manager "Ice Water" Joe Simmons suspended pitcher Doug Crothers for this incident, Crothers slugged the manager. Higgins miraculously recovered from his early travails and lack of support to post a 20-7 record.

On July 14, as the directors of the International League discussed the racial situation in Buffalo, the Newark Little Giants planned to send Stovey, their ace, to the mound in an exhibition game against the National League Chicago White Stockings. Once again manager Anson refused to field his squad if either Stovey or Walker appeared. Unlike 1883, Anson's will prevailed. On the same day, team owners, stating that "Many of the best players in the league are anxious to leave on account of the colored element," allowed current black players to remain but voted by a six-to-four margin to reject all future contracts with blacks. The teams with black players all voted against the measure, but Binghamton, which had just released Fowler and Renfroe, swung the vote in favor of exclusion.

Events in 1887 continued to conspire against black players. On September 11 the St. Louis Browns of the American Association refused to play a scheduled contest against the all-black Cuban Giants. "We are only doing what is right," they proclaimed. In November the Buffalo and Syracuse teams unsuccessfully attempted to lift the International League ban on blacks. The Ohio State League, which had fielded three black players, also adopted a rule barring additional contracts with blacks, prompting Welday Walker, who had appeared in the league, to protest, "The law is a disgrace to the present age. . . . There should be some broader cause—such as lack of ability, behavior and intelligence—for barring a player, rather than his color."

After 1887 only a handful of blacks appeared on integrated squads. Grant and Higgins returned to their original teams in 1888. Walker jumped from Newark to Syracuse. The following year only Walker remained for one final season, the last black in the International League until 1946. Richard Johnson, the erstwhile Dick Male, reappeared in the Ohio State League in 1888, and in 1889 joined Springfield in the Central Interstate League, where he hit 14 triples, stole 45 bases, and scored 100 runs in 100 games. In 1890 Harrisburg in the Eastern Interstate League fielded two blacks, and

Jamestown in the New York Penn League featured another. Bud Fowler and several other black players appeared in the Nebraska State League in 1892. Three years later Adrian in the Michigan State League signed five blacks, including Fowler and pitcher George Wilson, who posted a 29-4 record. Meanwhile, Sol White, who later chronicled these events in his 1906 book *The History of Colored Baseball,* played for Fort Wayne in the Western State League. In 1896 pitcher-outfielder Bert Jones joined Atchison in the Kansas State League, where he played for three seasons before being forced out in 1898. Almost fifty years would pass before another black would appear on an interracial club in organized baseball.

While integrated teams grew rare, several leagues allowed entry to all-black squads. In 1889 the Middle States League included the New York Gorhams and the Cuban Giants, the most famous black team of the age. The Giants posted a 55-17 record. In 1890 the alliance reorganized as the Eastern Interstate League and again included the Cuban Giants. Giants star George Williams paced the circuit with a .391 batting average, and teammate Arthur Thomas slugged 26 doubles and 10 triples, both league-leading totals. The Eastern Interstate League folded in midseason, and in 1891 the Giants made one final minor league appearance in the Connecticut State League. When this circuit also disbanded, the brief entry of the Cuban Giants in organized baseball came to an end. In 1898 a team calling itself the Acme Colored Giants affiliated with Pennsylvania's Iron and Oil League but won only eight of forty-nine games before dropping out, marking an ignoble conclusion to these early experiments in interracial play.

Overall, at least seventy blacks appeared in organized baseball in the late nineteenth century. About half played for all-black teams, the remainder for integrated clubs. Few lasted more than one season with the same team. By the 1890s the pattern for black baseball that would prevail for the next half century had emerged. Blacks were relegated to "colored" teams, playing most of their games on the barnstorming circuit, outside of any organized league structure. While exhibition contests allowed them to pit their skills against whites, they remained on the outskirts of baseball's mainstream, unheralded and unknown to most Americans.

As early as the 1880s and 1890s several all-black traveling squads had gained national reputations. The Cuban Giants, formed among the waiters of the Argyle Hotel to entertain guests in 1885, set the pattern and provided the recurrent nickname for these teams. Passing as Cubans, so as not to offend their white clientele, the Giants toured the East in a private railroad car, playing amateur and professional opponents. In the 1890s rivals like the Lincoln Giants from Nebraska, the Page Fence Giants from Michigan, and the Cuban X Giants in New York emerged. From the beginning these teams combined entertainment with their baseball to attract crowds. The Page Fence Giants, founded by Bud Fowler in 1895, would ride through the streets on bicycles to attract attention. In 1899 Fowler organized the All-American Black Tourists, who would arrive in full dress suits with opera hats and silk umbrellas. Their showmanship notwithstanding, the black teams of the 1890s included some of the best players in the nation. The Page Fence Giants won 118 of 154 games in 1895, with two of their losses coming against the major league Cincinnati Reds.

During the early years of the twentieth century many blacks still harbored hopes of regaining access to organized baseball. But even clandestine efforts to bring in blacks met a harsh fate. In 1901 Baltimore Orioles manager John McGraw attempted to pass second baseman Charlie Grant of the Columbia Giants off as an Indian named Chief Tokohama until Chicago White Sox president Charles Comiskey exposed the ruse.

In 1911 the Cincinnati Reds raised black hopes by signing two light-skinned Cubans, Armando Marsans and Rafael Almeida, prompting the *New York Age* to speculate, "Now that the first shock is over it would not be surprising to see a Cuban a few shades darker . . . breaking into the professional ranks . . . it would then be easier for colored players who are citizens of this country to get into fast company." But the Reds rushed to certify that Marsans and Almeida were "genuine Caucasians," and while light-skinned Cubans became a fixture in the majors, their darker brethren remained unwelcome. Over the years, tales circulated of United States blacks passing as Indians or Cubans but no documented cases exist.

Although most blacks lived in the South, during the first two decades of the twentieth century the great black teams and players congregated in the metropolises and industrial cities of the North. Chicago emerged as the primary center of black baseball with teams like the Leland Giants and the Chicago American Giants. In New York, the Lincoln Giants, which boasted pitching stars Smokey Joe Williams and Cannonball Dick Redding, shortstop John Henry Lloyd and catcher Louis Santop, reigned supreme. Other top clubs of the era included the Philadelphia Giants, the Hilldale Club (also of Philadelphia), the Indianapolis ABCs, and the Bacharach Giants of Atlantic City. Player contracts were nonexistent or nonbinding, and stars jumped frequently from team to team. "Wherever the money was," recalled John Henry Lloyd, "that's where I was."

Fans and writers often compared the great black players of this era to their white counterparts. Lloyd, one of the outstanding shortstops and hitters of that or any era, came to be known as "The Black Wagner," after his white contemporary Honus Wagner, who called it an "honor" and a "privilege" to be compared to the gangling black infielder. A St. Louis sportswriter, once said when asked who was the best player in baseball history, "If you mean in organized baseball, the answer would be Babe Ruth; but if you mean in all baseball . . . the answer would have to be a colored man named John Henry Lloyd." Pitcher "Rube" Foster earned his nickname by outpitching future Hall of Famer Rube Waddell, and Cuban Jose Mendez was called "The Black Matty," after Christy Mathewson.

The talents of Foster and Mendez notwithstanding, the greatest black pitcher of the early twentieth century was six-foot-five Smokey Joe Williams. Born in 1886, Williams spent a good part of his career pitching in his native Texas, unheralded until he joined the Leland Giants in 1909 at the age of twenty-four. From 1912 to 1923 he won renown as a strikeout artist for Harlem's Lincoln Giants. Against major league competition Williams won six games, lost four, and tied two, including a three-hit 1–0 victory over the National League champion Philadelphia Phillies in 1915. In 1925 he signed with the Homestead Grays and, although approaching his fortieth birthday, starred for seven more seasons. A 1952 poll to name the outstanding black pitcher of the half-century placed Williams in first place, ahead of the legendary Satchel Paige.

Oscar Charleston ranks as the greatest outfielder of the 1910s and 1920s. With tremendous speed and a strong, accurate arm, Charleston was the quintessential center fielder. During his fifteen-year career starting in 1915, Charleston hit for both power and average and may have been the most popular player of the 1920s. After he retired he managed the Philadelphia Stars, the Brooklyn Brown Dodgers, and other clubs.

Several major stars of this era labored outside the usual channels of black baseball. In 1914 white Kansas City promoter J. L. Wilkinson organized the All-Nations team, which included whites, blacks, Indians, Asians, and Latin Americans. Pitchers John Donaldson, Jose Mendez, and Bill Drake, and outfielder Cristobel Torriente played for the All-Nations team, described by one observer as "strong enough to give any major league team a nip-and-tuck battle." A black Army team from the Twenty-fifth Infantry Unit in Nogales, Arizona, featured pitcher Bullet Joe Rogan and shortstop Dobie Moore. In 1920, when Wilkinson formed the famed Kansas City Monarchs, the players from the All-Nations and the Twenty-fifth Infantry teams formed the nucleus of his club. In 1921 the Monarchs challenged the minor league Kansas City Blues to a tournament for the city championship. The Blues won the series five games to three. In 1922, however, the Monarchs won five of six games to claim boasting honors in Kansas City. One week later they swept a doubleheader from the touring Babe Ruth All-Stars.

In the years after 1910 Andrew "Rube" Foster emerged as the dominant figure in black baseball. Like many of his white contemporaries, Foster rose through the ranks of the national pastime—from star player to field manager to club owner. Born in Texas in 1879, Foster accepted an invitation to pitch for Chicago's Union Giants in 1902. By 1903 he was hurling for the Cuban X Giants against the Philadelphia Giants in a series billed as the "Colored Championship of the World." His four victories in a best-of-nine series clinched the title.

The following year, he had switched sides and registered two of three wins for the Philadelphia Giants in a similar match-up, striking out eighteen batters in one game and tossing a two-hitter in another. In 1907 he rejoined the Leland Giants and, in 1910, pitched for and managed a reconstituted team of that name to a 123-6 record.

As a pitcher, Foster had ranked among the nation's best; as a manager, his skills achieved legendary proportions. A master strategist and motivator, Foster's teams specialized in the bunt, the steal, and the hit and run, which came to characterize black baseball. Fans came to watch him sit on the bench, giving signs with a wave of his ever-present pipe. He became the friend and confidant of major league managers like John McGraw. Over the years, Foster trained a generation of black managers like Dave Malarcher, Biz Mackey, and Oscar Charleston in the subtleties of the game.

In 1911 Foster entered the ownership ranks, uniting with white saloon keeper John Schorling (the son-in-law of White Sox owner Charles Comiskey) to form the Chicago American Giants. With Schorling's financial backing, Foster's managerial acumen, a regular home field in Chicago, and high salaries, the American Giants attracted the best black players in the nation. Throughout the decade, whether barnstorming or hosting opponents in Chicago, the American Giants came to represent the pinnacle of black baseball.

By World War I, Foster dominated black baseball in Chicago and parts of the Midwest. In most other areas, however, white booking agents controlled access to stadiums and, as one newspaperman charged in 1917, "used circus methods to drag a bunch of our best citizens out, only to undergo humiliation . . . while [they sat] back and [grew] rich off a percentage of the proceeds." In the East, Nat Strong, the part owner of the Brooklyn Royal Giants, Philadelphia Giants, Cuban Stars, Cuban Giants, New York Black Yankees, and the renowned white semi-pro team, the Bushwicks, held a stranglehold on black competition. To break this monopoly and place the game more firmly under black control, Foster created the National Association of Professional Baseball Clubs, better known as the Negro National League, in 1920.

Foster's new organization marked the third attempt of the century to meld black teams into a viable league. In 1906 the International League of Independent Baseball Clubs, which had four black and two white teams, struggled through one season characterized by shifting and collapsing franchises. Four years later, Beauregard Moseley, secretary of Chicago's Leland Giants, attempted to form a National Negro Baseball League, but the association folded before a single game had been played.

The new Negro National League, which included the top teams from Chicago, St. Louis, Detroit, and other Midwestern cities, fared far better. At Foster's insistence, all clubs, with the exception of the Kansas City Monarchs, whom Foster reluctantly accepted, were controlled by blacks. J. L. Wilkinson, who owned the Monarchs, a major drawing card, had won the respect of his fellow owners and soon overcame Foster's reservations. He became the league secretary and Foster's trusted ally. Operating under the able guidance of Foster and Wilkinson, the league flourished during its early years. In 1923 it attracted four hundred thousand fans and accumulated two hundred thousand dollars in gate receipts.

The success of the Negro National League inspired competitors. In 1923 booking agent Nat Strong formed an Eastern Colored League, with teams in New York, Brooklyn, Baltimore, New Jersey, and Philadelphia. With four of the six teams owned by whites, and Strong controlling an erratic schedule, the league had somewhat less legitimacy than Foster's circuit. Playing in larger population centers, however, the more affluent Eastern clubs successfully raided some of the top players of the Negro National League before the circuits negotiated an uneasy truce in 1924. Throughout the remainder of the decade, however, acrimony rather than harmony characterized interleague relations. A third association emerged in the South, where the stronger independent teams in major cities formed the Southern Negro League. While this group became a breeding ground for top players, the impoverished nature of its clientele and the inability of clubs to bolster revenues with games against white squads rendered them unable to prevent their best players from jumping to the higher paying Northern teams.

At their best the Negro Leagues of the 1920s were haphazard affairs. Since most clubs continued to rely on barnstorming for their primary livelihood, scheduling proved difficult. Teams played uneven numbers of games and especially in the Eastern circuit skipped official contests for more lucrative nonleague matchups. Several of the stronger independent teams, like the Homestead Grays, remained unaffiliated. Umpires were often incompetent and lacked authority to control conditions. Finally, players frequently jumped from one franchise to another, peddling their services to the highest bidder. In 1926 Foster grew ill, stripping the Negro National League of his vital leadership. Two years later the Eastern Colored League disbanded, and in 1931 less than a year after Foster's death, the Negro National League departed the scene, once again leaving black baseball with no organized structure.

With the collapse of Foster's Negro National League and the onset of the Great Depression, the always-borderline economics of operating a black baseball club grew more precarious. White booking agents, like Philadelphia's Eddie Gottlieb or Abe Saperstein of the Midwest, again reigned supreme. In the early 1930s only the stronger independent clubs like the Homestead Grays or Kansas City Monarchs, novelty acts like the Cincinnati Clowns, or those teams backed by the "numbers kings" of the black ghettos could survive.

The Kansas City Monarchs emerged as the healthiest holdover from the old Negro National League. In 1929 owner Wilkinson had commissioned an Omaha, Nebraska, company to design a portable lighting system for night games. The equipment, consisting of a 250-horsepower motor and a 100-kilowatt generator, which illuminated lights atop telescoping poles fifty feet above the field, took about two hours to assemble. To pay for the innovation, Wilkinson mortgaged everything he owned and took in Kansas City businessman Tom Baird as a partner. But the gamble paid off. The novelty of night baseball allowed the Monarchs to play two and three games a day and made them the most popular touring club in the nation.

Meanwhile, in Pittsburgh, former basketball star Cumberland Posey, Jr., had forged the Homestead Grays into one of the best teams in America. Posey, the son of one of Pittsburgh's wealthiest black businessmen, had joined the Grays, then a sandlot team, as an outfielder in 1911. By the early 1920s he owned the club and began recruiting top national players to supplement local talent. In 1925 he signed thirty-nine-year-old Smokey Joe Williams, and the following year he lured Oscar Charleston. Over the next several seasons Posey recruited Judy Johnson, Martin Dihigo, and Cool Papa Bell. In 1930 he added a catcher from the Pittsburgh sandlots named Josh Gibson, and in 1934 brought in first baseman Buck Leonard from North Carolina. Unwilling to subject himself to outside control, Posey preferred to remain free from league affiliations. Yet for two decades, the Homestead Grays reigned as one of the strongest teams in black baseball.

In the 1930s Posey faced competition from crosstown rival Gus Greenlee, "Mr. Big" of Pittsburgh's North Side numbers rackets. Greenlee took over the Pittsburgh Crawfords, a local team, in 1930. Greenlee spent one hundred thousand dollars to build a new stadium, and wooed established ballplayers with lavish salary offers. In 1931 he landed the colorful Satchel Paige, the hottest young pitcher in the land, and the following year raided the Grays, outbidding Posey for the services of Charleston, Johnson, and Gibson. In 1934 James "Cool Papa" Bell jumped the St. Louis Stars and brought his legendary speed to the Crawfords. With five future Hall of Famers, Greenlee had assembled one of the great squads of baseball history.

The emergence of Gus Greenlee marked a new era for black baseball, the reign of the numbers men. In city after city, the numbers barons, seeking an element of respectability or an outlet to shield gambling profits from the Internal Revenue Service or merely the thrill of sports ownership, came to dominate black baseball.

In 1933 Greenlee unified the franchises owned by the numbers kings into a rejuvenated Negro National League. This "unholy alliance" sustained black baseball in the Northeast through depression and war. Even the collapse of the Crawfords and demolition of Greenlee Stadium in 1939 failed to weaken the league, which survived until the onset of integration. In 1937 a second circuit, the Negro American League, was formed in the Midwest and South. Dominated by Wilkinson and the Kansas City Monarchs, the Negro American League relied less on numbers brokers but more on white ownership for their financing.

The formation of the Negro American League encouraged the rejuvenation of an annual World Series, matching the champions of the two leagues. But the Negro League World Series never achieved the prominence of its white counterpart. The fact that league standings were often determined among teams playing uneven numbers of games diluted the notion of a champion. Furthermore, impoverished urban blacks could not sustain attendance at a prolonged series. As a result the Negro League World Series always took a back seat to the annual East-West All-Star Game played in Chicago. The East-West Game, originated by Greenlee in 1933, quickly emerged as the centerpiece of black baseball. Large crowds of blacks and whites watched the finest Negro League stars, and the revenues divided among the teams often spelled the difference between profit and loss at the season's end.

The impact of the Negro Leagues, however, ranged beyond the communities whose names the teams bore. Throughout the age of Jim Crow baseball, even in those years when a substantial league structure existed, official league games accounted for a relatively small part of the black baseball experience. Black teams would typically play over two hundred games a year, only a third of which counted in the league standings. The vast majority of contests occurred on the barnstorming circuit, pitting black athletes against a broad array of professional and semiprofessional competition, white and black, throughout the nation. In the pretelevision era, traveling teams brought a higher level of baseball to fans in the towns and cities of America and allowed local players to test their skills against the professionals. While some all-white teams like the "House of David" also trod the barnstorming trail, itinerancy was the key to survival for black squads. The capital needed to finance a Negro League team existed primarily in Northern cities, but the overwhelming majority of blacks lived in the South.

"The schedule was a rugged one," recalled Roy Campanella of the Baltimore Elite Giants. "Rarely were we in the same city two days in a row. Mostly we played by day and traveled by night." After the Monarchs introduced night baseball, teams played both day and night, appearing in two and sometimes three different ballparks on the same day. Teams traveled in buses—"our home, dressing room, dining room, and hotel"—or sandwiched into touring cars. "We had little time to waste on the road," states Quincy Trouppe, "so it was a rare treat when the cars would stop at times to let us stretch out and exercise for a few minutes." Most major hotels barred black guests, so even when the schedule allowed overnight stays, the athletes found themselves in less than comfortable accommodations. Large cities usually had better black hotels where ballplayers, entertainers, and other members of the black bourgeoisie congregated. On the road, however, Negro Leaguers more frequently were relegated to Jim Crow roadhouses, "continually under attack by bedbugs."

The black baseball experience extended beyond the confines of the United States and into Central America and the Caribbean. Negro Leaguers appeared regularly in the Cuban, Puerto Rican, Venezuelan, and Dominican winter leagues, where they competed against black and white Latin stars and major leaguers as well. Some blacks, like Willie Wells and Ray Dandridge, jumped permanently to the Mexican League, where several also became successful managers of interracial teams. As Wells explained, "I am not faced by the racial problem . . . I've found freedom and democracy here, something I never found in the United States . . . In Mexico, I am a man."

In the United States, however, blacks often found themselves in more distasteful roles. To attract crowds throughout the nation and to keep fans interested in the frequently one-sided contests against amateur competition, some black clubs injected elements of clowning and showmanship into their pregame and competitive performances. As early as the 1880s, comedy had characterized many barnstorming teams. Black baseball, even in its most serious form, tended to be flashier and less formal than white play. Against inferior teams, players often showboated and flaunted their superior skills. Pitcher Satchel Paige would call in his outfielders, or guarantee to strike out the first six or nine batters to face him, against semiprofessional squads. In the late 1930s Olympic star Jesse Owens traveled with the Monarchs, racing against horses in pregame exhibitions.

Black teams like the Tennessee Rats and Zulu Cannibals thrived on their minstrel show reputations. The most famous of these franchises were the "Ethiopian Clowns." Originating in Miami in the 1930s, the Clowns later operated out of Cincinnati and then Indianapolis. Their antics included a "pepperball and shadowball" performance (later emulated by basketball's Harlem Globetrotters), and midgame vaudeville routines by comics Spec Bebop, a dwarf, and King Tut. Players like Pepper Bassett, "the Rocking Chair Catcher" and "Goose" Tatum, a talented first baseman and natural comedian, enlivened the festivities. By the 1940s, the Clowns, through the effort of booking agent Syd Pollack, dominated the baseball comedy market. In 1943 their popularity won the Clowns entrance into the Negro Leagues, although other owners demanded they drop the demeaning "Ethiopian" nickname. Although never one of the better black teams, the Clowns greatly bolstered Negro League attendance.

Their popularity notwithstanding, the comedy teams reflected one of the worst elements of black baseball. The Clowns and Zulus perpetuated stereotypes drawn from Stepin Fetchit and Tarzan movies. "Negroes must realize the danger in insisting that ballplayers paint their faces and go through minstrel show revues before each ballgame," protested sportswriter Wendell Smith. Many black players resented the image that all were clowns. "Didn't nobody clown in our league but the Indianapolis Clowns," objected Piper Davis. "We played baseball."

Even without the clowning, black baseball offered a more freewheeling and, in many respects, more exciting brand of baseball than the major leagues. Since the 1920s, when Babe Ruth had revolutionized the game, the majors had pursued power strategies, emphasizing the home run above all else. Although the great sluggers of the Negro Leagues rivaled those in the National and American Leagues, they comprised but one element in the speed-dominated universe of "tricky baseball." Black teams emphasized the bunt, the stolen base, and the hit and run. "We played by the 'coonsbury' rules," boasted second baseman Newt Allen. "That's just any way you think you can win, any kind of play you think you could get by on." In games between white and black all-star teams, this style of play often confounded the major leaguers. Center fielder James "Cool Papa" Bell personified this approach. Bell was so fast, marveled rival third baseman Judy Johnson, "You couldn't play back in your regular position or you'd never throw him out." In one game against a major league All-Star squad, Bell scored from first base on a sacrifice bunt! In center field, his great speed allowed him to lurk in the shallow reaches of the outfield, ranging great distances to make spectacular catches.

Since most rosters included only fourteen to eighteen men, Negro League players demonstrated a wide range of versatility. Each was required to fill in at a variety of positions. Star pitchers often found themselves in the outfield when not on the mound. Some won renown at more than one position. Ted "Double-Duty" Radcliffe often pitched in the first game of a doubleheader and caught in the second. Cuban Martin Dihigo, whom many rank as the greatest player of all time, excelled at every position. In 1938, in the Mexican League, he led the league's pitchers with an 18-2 record and the league's hitters with a .387 average.

The manpower shortage offered opportunities for individuals to display their all-around talents, but it also limited the competitiveness of the black teams. While on a given day a Negro League franchise, featuring one of its top pitchers, might defeat a major league squad, most teams lacked the depth to compete on a regular basis. "The big leagues were strong in every position," remarks Radcliffe. "Most of the colored teams had a few stars but they weren't strong in every position."

While black teams may not have matched the top clubs in organized baseball, the individual stars of the 1930s and 1940s clearly ranked among the best of any age. Homestead Gray teammates Josh Gibson and Buck Leonard won renown as the Babe Ruth and Lou Gehrig of the Negro Leagues. The Grays discovered Gibson in 1929 as an eighteen-year-old catcher on the sandlots of Pittsburgh, where he had already earned a reputation for five-hundred-foot home runs. For seventeen years he launched prodigious blasts off pitchers in the Negro Leagues, on the barnstorming tour, and in Latin America. As talented as any major league star, Gibson died in January 1947 at age thirty-five, just three months before Jackie Robinson joined the Brooklyn Dodgers. Leonard, four years older than Gibson, starred in both the Negro and Mexican Leagues as a sure-handed, power-hitting first baseman. The Newark Eagles in the early 1940s boasted the "million dollar infield" of first baseman Mule Suttles, second baseman Dick Seay, shortstop Willie Wells, and third baseman Ray Dandridge. The acrobatic fielding skills of Seay, Wells, and Dandridge led Roy Campanella to call this the greatest infield he ever saw.

Amidst the many talented Negro Leaguers of 1930s and 1940s, however, one long, lean figure came to personify black baseball to blacks and whites alike. Leroy "Satchel" Paige began his prolonged athletic odyssey in his hometown in 1924 as a seventeen-year-old pitcher with the semiprofessional Mobile Tigers. He joined the Chattanooga Black Lookouts of the Negro Southern League in 1926. Two years later, the Lookouts sold his contract to the Birmingham Black Barons. By 1930 his explosive fastball, impeccable control, and eccentric mannerisms had made him a legend in the South. In 1932 Gus Greenlee brought Paige to the Pittsburgh Crawfords where the colorful pitcher embellished his reputation by winning fifty-four games in his first two years. Greenlee also began the practice of hiring out Paige to semiprofessional clubs that needed a one-day box office boost.

For seven years Paige feuded with Greenlee, jumping the club when a better offer appeared, being banished "for life," and then returning. In the mid-1930s, in addition to his stints with the Crawfords, Paige won fame by boosting Bismarck, North Dakota, to the national semiprofessional championships, hurling for the Dominican Republic at the behest of dictator Rafael Trujillo, in the Mexican League, and especially on the postseason barnstorming trail pitted against Dizzy Dean's Major League All-Stars. "That skinny old Satchel Paige with those long arms is my idea of the pitcher with the greatest stuff I ever saw," claimed the unusually immodest Dean.

Paige's appeal stemmed as much from his unusual persona as his pitching prowess. A born showman, Paige's lanky, lackadaisical presence evoked popular racial stereotypes of the age. "As undependable as a pair of sec-ondhand suspenders," Paige often arrived late or failed to show. His names for his pitches (the "bee ball" which buzzed and all of a sudden, "be there"; the "jump ball"; and the "trouble ball") and his minstrel show one-liners enhanced the image. But on the mound Paige invariably rose to the occasion against top competition or challenged inferior opponents by calling in the outfield or promising to strike out the side.

In 1938 a sore arm threatened to curtail Paige's career, but the Kansas City Monarchs, hoping his reputation alone would draw fans, signed him for their traveling second team. On the road, Paige perfected a repertoire of curves and off-speed pitches, including his famous "hesitation" pitch. When his fastball returned in 1939, he became a better pitcher than ever. Promoted to the main Monarch club, Paige pitched the team to four consecutive Negro American League pennants. From 1941 to 1947, although officially still a Monarch, Paige spent far more time as an independent performer, hired out by Monarchs' owner J. L. Wilkinson to semi-pro and Negro League clubs. "He kept our league going," recalls Othello Renfroe. "Anytime a team got into trouble, it sent for Satchel to pitch." Paige also continued to hurl against major league All-Star teams. In the 1940s the example of Satchel Paige, whose legend had spread into the white community, offered the most compelling argument for the desegregation of the national pastime.

Paige's exploits against white players revealed a fundamental irony about baseball in the Jim Crow era. While organized baseball rigidly enforced its ban on black players within the major and minor leagues, opportunities abounded for black athletes to prove themselves against white competition along the unpoliced boundaries of the national pastime. During the 1930s Western promoters sponsored tournaments for the best semiprofessional teams in the nation. These squads often featured former and future major leaguers as well as top local talent. In 1934 the *Denver Post* tourney, "the little World Series of the West," invited the Kansas City Monarchs to compete for the $7,500 first prize. The Monarchs fought their way into the finals against the House of David team (also owned by J. L. Wilkinson) only to find themselves confronted on the mound by Paige, rented out to pitch this one game. Paige outdueled Monarchs ace Chet Brewer, 2–1. Black teams became a fixture in the *Post* series, emerging victorious for several consecutive years.

In 1935 the National Baseball Congress began an annual tournament in Wichita, Kansas. The competition attracted community squads heartily bankrolled by local business leaders. Neil Churchill, an auto dealer from Bismarck, North Dakota, recruited a half-dozen black stars, including Paige and Brewer, to represent the town in the Wichita competition. Bismarck naturally swept the series, and thereafter teams that were either integrated or all black routinely appeared in the National Baseball Congress invitational each year.

In an age in which the major leagues were confined to the East and Midwest, and television had yet to bring baseball into people's homes, postseason tours by big league stars offered yet another opportunity for black players to prove their equality on the diamond. Games pitting blacks against whites were popular features of the barnstorming circuit. Until the late 1920s, when Commissioner Kenesaw Mountain Landis limited postseason play to all-star squads, black teams frequently met and defeated major league clubs in postseason competition. During the next decade, matchups between the Babe Ruth or Dizzy Dean All-Stars and black players became frequent. In the autumn of 1934 and 1935, Dean's team traveled the nation accompanied by the "Satchel Paige All-Stars." In one memorable 1934 game, called by baseball executive Bill Veeck "the greatest pitching battle I have ever seen," Paige bested Dean 1–0. Surviving records of interracial contests during the 1930s reveal that blacks won two-thirds of the games. "That's when we played the hardest," asserted Judy Johnson, "to let them know, and to let the public know, that we had the same talent they did and probably a little better at times."

The rivalries proved particularly keen on the West Coast, where Monarchs co-owner Tom Baird organized the California Winter League, which included black teams, white major and minor league stars, and some of Mexico's top players. In 1940 pitcher Chet Brewer formed the Kansas City Royals, which each year fielded one of the best clubs on the coast. One year the Royals defeated the Hollywood Stars, who had won the Pacific Coast League championship, six straight times. In 1945 Brewer's team, including Jackie Robinson and Satchel Paige, regularly defeated major league competition.

The most famous of the interracial barnstorming tours occurred in 1946, when Cleveland Indian pitcher Bob Feller organized a major league all-star team, rented two Flying Tiger aircraft and hopped the nation accompanied by the Satchel Paige All-Stars. With Feller and Paige each pitching a few innings a day, the tour proved extremely lucrative for promoters and players alike and gave widespread publicity to the skills of the black athletes.

The World War II years marked the heyday of the Negro Leagues. With black and white workers flooding into Northern industrial centers, with relatively full employment, and with a scarcity of available consumer goods, attendance at all sorts of entertainment events increased dramatically. In 1942 three million fans saw Negro League teams play, and the East-West game in 1943 attracted over fifty-one thousand fans. "Even the white folks was coming out big," recalled Satchel Paige.

But World War II also generated forces that would challenge the foundations of Jim Crow baseball. In the armed forces, baseball teams like the Black Bluejackets of the Great Lakes Naval Station team posted outstanding records against teams featuring white major leaguers. In 1945 a well-publicized tournament of teams in the European theater featured top black players like Leon Day, Joe Green, and Willard Brown in the championship round. More significantly, the hypocrisy of blacks fighting for their country but unable to participate in the national pastime grew steadily more apparent. As wartime manpower shortages forced major league teams to rely on a fifteen-year-old pitcher, over-the-hill veterans, and one-armed Pete Gray, their refusal to sign black players seemed increasingly irrational. "How do you think I felt when I saw a one-armed outfielder?" moaned Chet Brewer. Pitcher Nate Moreland protested, "I can play in Mexico, but I have to fight for America where I can't play." Pickets at Yankee Stadium carried placards asking, "If we are able to stop bullets, why not balls?"

Amidst this heightened awareness, organized baseball repeatedly walked to the precipice of integration but always failed to take the final leap. In 1942 Moreland and All-American football star Jackie Robinson requested a tryout at a White Sox training camp in Pasadena, California. Robinson, in particular, impressed White Sox manager Jimmy Dykes but nothing came of the event. Brooklyn Dodger manager Leo Durocher publicly stated his willingness to sign blacks, only to receive a stinging rebuke from Commissioner Landis. Landis again short-circuited integration talk the following year. At the annual baseball meetings, black leaders, led by actor Paul Robeson, gained the opportunity to address major league owners on the issue, but Landis ruled all further discussion out of order.

In 1943 several minor and major league teams were rumored close to signing black players. In California, where winter league play had demonstrated the potential of black players, several clubs considered integration. The Los Angeles Angels of the Pacific Coast League announced tryouts for three black players, but pressure from other league owners doomed the plan. Oakland owner Vince DeVicenzi ordered Manager Johnny Vergez to consider pitcher Chet Brewer, the most popular black player on the West Coast, for the Oaks. Vergez refused and the issue died. Two years later Bakersfield, a Cleveland Indian farm team in the California League, offered Brewer a position as player-coach, but the parent club vetoed the plan.

At the major league level, Washington Senators owner Clark Griffith called sluggers Josh Gibson and Buck Leonard into his office and asked if they would like to play in the major leagues. They answered affirmatively but never heard from Griffith again. In Pittsburgh, *Daily Worker* sports editor Nat Low pressured Pirate owner William Benswanger to arrange a tryout for catcher Roy Campanella and pitcher Dave Barnhill. At the last minute Benswanger canceled the audition, citing "unnamed pressures."

For more than two decades, the imperial Landis had reigned over baseball as an implacable foe of integration. While hypocritically denying the existence of any "rule, formal or informal, or any understanding— unwritten, subterranean, or sub-anything—against the signing of Negro players," Landis had stringently policed the color line. His death in 1944 removed a major barrier for integration advocates.

In April 1945, with World War II entering its final months, the integration crusade gained momentum. On April 6, *People's Voice* sportswriter Joe Bostic appeared at the Brooklyn Dodger training camp at Bear Mountain, New York, with two Negro League players, Terris McDuffie and Dave "Showboat" Thomas, and demanded a tryout. An outraged but outmaneuvered Dodger president Branch Rickey allowed the pair to work out with the club. One week later, a more serious confrontation occurred in Boston. The Red Sox, under pressure from popular columnist Dave Egan and city councilman Isidore Muchnick, agreed to audition Sam Jethroe, the Negro League's leading hitter in 1944, second baseman Marvin Williams, and Kansas City Monarch shortstop Jackie Robinson, all top prospects in their mid-twenties. The Fenway Park tryout, however, proved little more than a formality, and the players never again heard from the Red Sox.

The publicity surrounding these events, however, forced the major leagues to address the issue at its April meetings. At the urging of black sportswriter Sam Lacy, Leslie O'Connor, Landis's interim successor, established the Major League Committee on Baseball Integration in April 1945 to review the problem. In addition, the racial views of newly appointed Commissioner A. B. "Happy" Chandler came under close scrutiny. A former governor of the segregated state of Kentucky, Chandler nonetheless offered at least verbal support to the entry of blacks into organized ball. "If a black boy can make it on Okinawa and Guadalcanal, hell, he can make it in baseball," Chandler told black reporter Rick Roberts. Whether Chandler, however, unlike Landis, would reinforce his rhetoric with positive actions remained uncertain.

Unbeknownst to the integration advocates, baseball officials, and local politicians sand-dancing around the race issue, Branch Rickey, the president of the Brooklyn Dodgers, had already set in motion the events that would lead to the historic breakthrough.

SIX

Unreconciled Strivings

Baseball in Jim Crow America

Andrew "Rube" Foster epitomized African-American pride. A tall, imposing, right-handed pitcher, he had migrated from his native Texas to Chicago in 1902 to play for the Chicago Union Giants. When warned that he might face "the best clubs in the land, white clubs," he announced, "I fear nobody." Over the next decade he established himself as perhaps the outstanding pitcher in all of baseball. In 1911 he formed his own team, the Chicago American Giants, and won a reputation as a managerial genius equal to his friend, John McGraw. Nine years later Foster, seeking to "keep colored baseball from control of the whites" and "to do something concrete for the loyalty of the Race," created the Negro National League. Foster criticized white owners for not letting African Americans "count a ticket [or] learn anything about the business," and called for a league dominated by black men. "There can be no such thing as [a black baseball league] with four or five of the directors white any more than you can call a streetcar a steamship," he asserted. Foster urged black fans: "It is your league. Nurse it! Help it! Keep it!" Yet Foster's intense racial pride notwithstanding, he also made his ultimate goal clear. "We have to be ready," he proclaimed, "when the time comes for integration."[1]

Rube Foster—and indeed, the entire experience of blacks in baseball in early-twentieth-century America[2]—exemplifies elements of Booker T. Washington's call for the development of separate economic spheres so that his race might prepare itself for ultimate inclusion in American life. Yet black baseball also captured what Washington's rival, W. E. B. Du Bois, labeled the "twoness" of the African-American experience. "One ever feels his twoness—an American, a Negro," wrote Du Bois, "two souls, two thoughts, two unreconciled strivings; two warring ideals in one dark body, whose dogged strength alone keeps it from being torn asunder." The architects of black baseball embodied this dualism. They strove to create viable enterprises that served their communities and simultaneously might win a measure of respectability in the broader society. These ventures would prepare them for the day on which, according to Du Bois's vision, it would be "possible for a man to be both a Negro and American, without being cursed and spit upon by his fellows, without having the doors of Opportunity closed roughly in his face."[3]

The essence of black professional baseball is far more elusive than that of its white counterpart. The major leagues always constituted the epitome and cultural core of mainstream baseball, but the formal Negro Leagues represented no more than a segment of the black baseball experience. No leagues existed until 1920, and even during their halcyon days official contests never constituted more than perhaps a third of the games played. Some of the strongest black teams and best players performed outside the league structure. Top teams often boasted names like the Homestead Grays, Bachrach Giants, or the Hilldale Club, reflecting affiliations not to major cities but to people and smaller communities. The most popular attractions often involved exhibitions against white semiprofessional and professional teams. In all of these many guises and varieties, black baseball constituted a vital element of African-American culture, while also dramatizing the contradictions and challenges of survival in a world dominated by whites.

Within the African-American community, the officials, players, and teams of black baseball symbolized pride and achievement while creating a sphere of style and excitement that overlapped with the worlds of black business, politics, religion, and entertainment. During the baseball season Negro League teams constituted a constant presence in the black community. Placards announcing the games appeared in the windows of local businesses, along with advertisements featuring player endorsements and commands to "get those pretty clothes" for the "opening day . . . Fashion Parade."[4] In Kansas City fans could purchase tickets in a number of locales where African Americans congregated, including the Monarch Billiard Parlor, Stark's Newspaper Stand, the Panama Taxi Stand, and McCampbell's and Hueston's Drug Store. The Elbon and Lincoln movie theaters would show pictures of the players, advertisements for the games, and newsreel footage of the lavish opening day ceremonies.[5]

Local businesses rallied around the team. Some, like Herman Stark's clothing store in Detroit, offered prizes to the first player to hit a home run or get a hit in a Sunday or opening day contest.[6] Several cities featured booster clubs, like the Hilldale Royal Rooters and Baltimore's Frontiers Club, that supported their teams. The Kansas City Booster Club, the most lavish of these organizations, included both black and white merchants whose stores served the black community. Formed in 1926, the Kansas City Boosters organized the opening day parade, sponsored banquets for the players, and staged beauty contests at the ball game.[7] These businesses profited, in turn, from black baseball. "The cafes, beer joints, and rooming houses of the Negro neighborhoods all benefited as black baseball monies sometimes trickled, sometimes rippled through the black community," writes Donn Rogosin. After the 1944 East-West All-Star Game in Chicago, reported Wendell Smith, "Hot spots were all loaded, and so were most of the patrons."[8]

African-American baseball also provided one of the most popular features of black newspapers. As early as the turn of the century the *Indianapolis Freeman* had discovered that baseball coverage attracted readers. Sportswriter David Wyatt, who had played for the Cuban Giants and Chicago Union Giants from 1896 to 1902, reported on news of black baseball from all over the country. The Indianapolis ABCs and other teams would arrange matches by placing ads in the *Freeman*.[9] Other black weeklies began covering the game more seriously after 1910. The *Philadelphia Tribune* forged a close alliance with Ed Bolden's Hilldale Club. Bolden advertised games in the *Tribune* and provided press releases and game results. Beginning in 1914 the *Tribune* began to print box scores and in 1915 published Bolden's weekly column, "Hilldale Pickups."[10] Black newspapermen, led by Wyatt, played key roles in the creation and promotion of the Negro National League in 1920. "Behind this opening should be the concentrated support of every race man in Detroit," asserted the *Detroit Contender*. "If the league succeeds your race succeeds; if the league fails, the race fails. . . . Our ability to put over large projects will be measured largely by the way we handle this one."[11]

Nonetheless, reporting in the African-American journals was frequently sketchy. Black newspapers could not afford to send writers to accompany clubs on the road and depended heavily on reports submitted by the teams. This source proved highly unreliable, and the traveling squads often failed to call in or refused to reveal losses. In addition, since many of the black weeklies appeared on Saturday, they tended to focus on previews of the following day's contests, rather than results of the previous week, making it difficult for fans to follow a team with any consistency. Nonetheless, by the 1920s and 1930s all the major black weeklies had substantial sports sections with regular coverage and standout columnists like Frank A. (Fay) Young of the *Chicago Defender*, Wendell Smith of the *Pittsburgh Courier*, and Sam Lacy of the *Baltimore Afro-American*. The black press played a critical role in promoting the East-West All-Star Game, the showcase event of Negro League baseball. The newspapers printed ballots and lists of eligible players, and by 1939 top performers received as many as five hundred thousand votes. "The success of the game was made by Negro newspapers," commented Fay Young. "It was the Negro press that carried the percentages, the feats of the various stars all through the year, and it was the readers of the Negro newspapers who had knowledge of what they were going to see."[12]

Owners and officials of black clubs often ranked among the most prominent figures in the African-American community. Club officials participated actively in local business, fraternal, and civil rights organizations. Ed Bolden, owner of the Philadelphia-based Hilldale Club in the 1920s, belonged to local black fraternal groups and the Citizen's Republican Club. Kansas City Monarchs' secretary Quincy J. Gilmore was the guiding force behind the local Elks Club and the Negro Twilight League that brought together industrial, youth, and semiprofessional teams in the Kansas City area. Homestead Grays owner Cum Posey served on the Homestead school board.[13] Bolden, Posey, Rube Foster, and others wrote regular columns for local black newspapers.

Several team owners figured prominently in civil rights activities. Olivia Taylor, who inherited the Indianapolis ABCs from her husband, became president of the Indianapolis NAACP chapter in 1925.[14] Newark Eagle owner Effa Manley was an indefatigable campaigner against discrimination. In the years before she and her husband Abe purchased the ball club, Manley had achieved prominence in New York City as the secretary of the Citizen's League for Fair Play, which waged successful campaigns against Harlem businesses that refused to employ African Americans. In Newark Manley served as the treasurer of the New Jersey chapter of the NAACP and on several occasions held ballpark benefits for the organization. At one event the Eagles sold NAACP "Stop Lynching" buttons to fans. Manley also joined the "Citizen's Committee to End Jim Crow in Baseball Committee" created by the Congress of Industrial Organizations in 1942.[15]

Black teams hosted numerous benefit games for African-American charities and causes, raising funds for churches, hospitals, youth groups, and civil rights bodies. The Kansas City Monarchs staged benefits for the Negro National Business League and the Red Cross. The Newark Eagles regularly raised money to purchase medical equipment for the Booker T. Washington Community Hospital. During World War I the Indianapolis ABCs and Chicago American Giants played games on behalf of the Red Cross, and in the 1920s Hilldale played fund-raisers for war veterans. The first black baseball game at Yankee Stadium pitted the Lincoln Giants and Baltimore Black Sox in a 1930 benefit for the Brotherhood of Sleeping Car Porters. The outbreak of World War II prompted additional efforts.[16]

The players themselves often had close ties to the cities in which they performed. Many teams recruited from the local sandlots and discovered some of their best players literally perched on their doorsteps. Hall of Fame outfielder Oscar Charleston, who grew up on Indianapolis's East Side, served as a batboy for the ABCs before joining the squad as a player. He performed alongside Frank Warfield, "the pride of Indianapolis's West Side." The Homestead Grays discovered Josh Gibson playing semiprofessional baseball in Pittsburgh's Hill district. Memphis Blues pitching ace Verdell Mathis grew up within a short walk of Martin Field. Effa Manley's Eagles frequently found their best players—including Monte Irvin, Larry Doby, and Don Newcombe—in the Newark area.[17] The Birmingham Black Barons snatched the fifteen-year-old Willie Mays from a local high school.

The players often made the Negro League cities their year-round homes and became fixtures in their communities. In Detroit in the 1920s players found winter jobs in the local automobile plants. Turkey Stearnes and other Detroit Stars worked in factories owned by Detroit Tigers co-owner Walter O. Briggs, glad to hire them in his legendarily grimy and unsafe paint shops, but not on his baseball team. In Pittsburgh many of the Crawfords found work as lookouts for owner Gus Greenlee's gambling operations.[18] Some athletes stayed on in the cities where they had won their fame, opening up bars and other small businesses. John Henry "Pop" Lloyd, who had played for, among other teams, the Bachrach Giants of Atlantic City, settled there on retirement and reigned as "a sort of foster father" to the city's children. Lloyd became the commissioner of the local little league and had a neighborhood ball field named in his honor.[19]

Those who did not have homes in the city often resided during the season at the finest black hotels. In an age when most mainstream hotels even in northern cities barred African Americans, each major city featured a showplace hotel where traveling athletes, entertainers, and members of the black elite lodged and congregated. These were the places, as poet Amiri Baraka describes Newark's Grand Hotel, where "the ballplayers and the slick people could meet."[20] In Detroit the players stayed at the Norwood, which also housed the Plantation nightclub. In Baltimore the Black Sox lived at the Smith Hotel, owned by the city's black Democratic political boss. Street's Hotel in Kansas City, located at Eighteenth and Vine Streets, was the place, according to its manager, that "everybody that came to KC stopped at."[21]

As a teenager in Newark, Baraka reveled in mixing with the postgame throngs at the Grand Hotel, where "Everybody's super clean and high-falutin'." Monte Irvin recalls, "To the fans, the hotel presented an opportunity to join the ballplayers' special circle."[22] This circle often included not just ballplayers, but the entertainment royalty of black America—jazz musicians, dancers, actors and actresses, theater and movie stars, and boxers like Jack Johnson and Joe Louis. Indeed, a close bond formed between the itinerant athletes and performers. Entertainers often could be found at the ballparks, rooting for their favorite clubs and clowning around with their favorite players. The Mills Brothers loved to don Pittsburgh Crawford uniforms and work out with the club. When they appeared at team owner Gus Greenlee's Crawford Grille, Satchel Paige, a talented singer, would return the favor, joining them on stage for impromptu jazz sessions. In Memphis, where Martin Park bordered the Beale Street music district, bluesman B. B. King would set up near first base and sing as the fans filed in. Lena Horne, whose father was Gus Greenlee's right-hand man, appeared frequently at Negro League games. The New York Black Yankees, co-owned by dancer Bill "Bojangles" Robinson, attracted a parade of celebrities to games at Dyckman's Oval in Harlem. When Count Basie was in Kansas City on a Sunday, he headed out to see the Monarchs, "because that's where everyone else was going on a Sunday afternoon."[23]

The games themselves, particularly season openers and Sunday games, were festive occasions in the black community. As the *Chicago Defender* reported in 1923, fans would turn out for the first home game "like a lot of bees hidden away all winter . . . getting active when the sun shines."[24] The contests often marked the culmination of daylong celebrations. David Wyatt, a former player turned sports reporter, described the scene in Indianapolis in 1917:

> The big noise, the mammoth street parade, swung into motion promptly at ten o'clock upon Saturday. There were something like one hundred conveyances of the gasoline, electric or other propelling types in the line . . . occupied by persons of both races, some internationally known to fame. . . . [We] jammed the downtown district and went on our way rejoicing.[25]

In Kansas City the Monarchs' Booster Club organized an annual parade that snaked through the city's black district and arrived at the park in time for the opening ceremonies.[26] These ceremonies in most cities featured high school bands, color guards, prominent black celebrities, or black and white politicians to throw out the first pitch.

Indeed, as the African-American citizenry in northern cities expanded in numbers and influence, baseball stadiums became a prime location for politicians courting the black vote. In Atlantic City in the 1920s the

Bachrach Giants were named for Mayor Henry Bachrach, who had brought an African-American team up from Florida to entertain the resort town's growing population of black hotel workers. Playing at a converted dog track near the Boardwalk, the Bachrach Giants became a popular fixture and an advertisement for the mayor for the remainder of the decade. Indiana Governor Harry Leslie, hoping to rebuild black support for the Republicans in the wake of the party's flirtation with the Ku Klux Klan, threw out the first pitch at the ABCs home opener in 1930.[27] Although attendance by governors proved rare, in the 1930s and 1940s big-city mayors routinely kicked off the local black season. When Pittsburgh Crawfords' owner Gus Greenlee unveiled his new stadium in 1932, the mayor, city council, and county commissioner all attended. In 1935 Mayor Fiorello La Guardia performed the first-pitch honors at a Brooklyn Eagles–Homestead Grays game, and Cleveland Mayor Harry L. Davis joined eight thousand fans at a match between the Crawfords and American Giants honoring Ohio State track star Jesse Owens. The mayors of Baltimore, Kansas City, and Newark all frequently appeared at opening games. The mayor of Newark, recalls Jerry Izenberg, could avoid the Eagles' home opener only "if he chose not to be reelected."[28]

Opening day and Sunday contests attracted a wide cross section of the African-American community, dressed in their finest clothes. A white writer who attended a Sunday game in Detroit in 1922 reported, "All the youth, beauty, and chivalry of local African aristocracy is there to see and be seen. The latest 'modes and the most advanced fashions in "nobby suitings for young men" are on view'. . . . Gallons of perfumery and tons of powder are expended on this great social event." The tradition continued into the 1940s. Memphis blues/soul singer Rufus Thomas recalls: "They put on their best frocks, the best suits, the best everything they had and went to the ball game and when they would sit up there watching the game, it looked like a fashion parade." For a rookie pitcher, like Newark's James Walker, the intimidating scene "looked like a big cloud of flowers of different colors."[29]

The Sunday spectacle, according to Newark resident Connie Woodruff, represented "a combination of two things, an opportunity for all women to show off their Sunday finery" and "a once a week family affair." People would arrive, according to Woodruff, "with big baskets of chicken, potato salad, all the things you would have on a picnic . . . it was the thrill of being there, being seen, seeing who they could see."[30] For recent arrivals from the South, Sunday games often served as reunions. Lena Cox, the sister of Homestead Grays' star Buck Leonard, had migrated from Rocky Mount, North Carolina, to Washington DC. "You would see everyone from home when you went to the ball game," she recalled. Many people went directly from church to the ballpark. Clubs often played benefit games for churches and gave free passes to ministers, who, in return, urged their flocks to accompany them to the games. In Washington DC, where Elder Michaux operated a popular church across the street from Griffith Stadium, his parishioners would cross Georgia Avenue to catch the Homestead Grays in action during the 1940s after the service.[31]

The Sunday games, asserted Black Yankees outfielder Charlie Biot, "were THE event of the week." Teams capitalized on the popularity of these contests by throwing their star pitchers and scheduling four-team doubleheaders. According to an intimate of Rube Foster, Foster commanded Negro National League affiliates in the 1920s that "no star twirler was used to the limit before a small Saturday crowd with the prospects of a good Sunday attendance." In Memphis in the 1940s ace Verdell Mathis became known as the "Sunday Feature," because he almost always hurled the first game of the scheduled doubleheader.[32]

This emphasis on Sunday games, however, also revealed the limitations of black baseball. The black professional game depended, as Janet Bruce has written, "on an impoverished people who had too little discretionary money and too little leisure time."[33] As most blacks who could afford to attend games worked or searched for casual work six days a week, Sunday was often the only day they could attend games. Sunday matchups usually attracted between four thousand and eight thousand fans; weekday contests drew a few hundred. As Foster noted, "There are only twenty-seven Sundays and holidays in the playing season. It is a proven fact that on Sundays only have clubs been able to play at a profit. The weekdays have on many occasions been a complete loss."[34] Since several states, most notably Pennsylvania, had "blue laws" prohibiting Sunday games, teams like the Hilldale Club lost these lucrative home dates. Teams that shared facilities with white major and minor league squads could only schedule home Sunday dates when the host club was on the road. A few Sunday rainouts could devastate a team's narrow profit margin.

Attempts to stage a World Series between the champions of the Negro National League and the Eastern Colored League in 1924 illustrated the problem. Since black fans in any city could not be expected to afford tickets for more than a few consecutive games, the ten-game series pitting the Hilldale Club against the Monarchs was played not just in Philadelphia and Kansas City, but in Baltimore and Chicago as well. Three Sunday dates attracted an average of almost 7,000 fans a game. Two Monday games, including the finale to a tightly contested series, attracted crowds of 534 and 1,549. This pattern continued into the 1930s and 1940s. The Newark Eagles, for example, averaged 4,293 Sunday admissions in 1940, but only 870 on other days.[35]

These realities of black baseball exposed a great deal about the complex racial dynamics of America. As early as 1911 David Wyatt pointed out that "baseball can not live or thrive upon the attendance of colored only," and noted the necessity of scheduling weekday games against white teams. As Neil Lanctot demonstrates, the success of the Hilldale Club in the early 1920s stemmed from the availability of white opponents. Hilldale played almost two-thirds of its games against white semiprofessional and industrial teams.[36]

White baseball fans across the nation attended games that pitted black teams against white semiprofessional and professional squads, but most whites had minimal exposure to top-level competition between black athletes. The daily press in most cities rarely covered constructive black activities of any kind. When several white papers deigned to mention the 1924 Negro World Series, the *Kansas City Call* observed, "Negro sport has done what Negro Churches, Negro lodges, Negro business could not do . . . shown that a Negro can get attention for a good deed well done, and that publicity is no longer the exclusive mark of our criminals." In the 1930s and 1940s Effa Manley discovered that "it was next to impossible to get much space in the white metropolitan dailies."[37] Reports of games that found their way into the white press often lampooned the fans and festivities or referred to the players as "duskies" and other racist terms.

White fans appear to have been more likely to attend all-black games in the early years of the century. In 1907 a three-game series in Chicago between the Indianapolis ABCs and Lincoln Giants attracted 30,000 fans of both races. "There was no color line anywhere; our white brethren outnumbered us by a few hundred, and bumped elbows in the grandstands . . . the box seats and bleachers," reported Wyatt. The ABCs, Monarchs, Hilldales, and Lincoln Giants (who played in Harlem) all reported substantial white attendance during these years.[38] During the 1920s however, perhaps due to the more rigid segregation arising in response to the Great Migration and 1919 race riots, white attendance dropped to 10 percent or less. Efforts to bolster profits by attracting more whites inevitably proved unsuccessful. In 1939 Effa Manley made a strong effort to lure whites to Newark Eagles' games, but the *Philadelphia Tribune* reported in 1940 that "Up in Newark . . . [one] would have seen 95 colored faces for every five white ones." Chicago reporter Fay Young frequently criticized attempts to get more whites to the games. Although the leagues had employed white promoters to bolster attendance at all-star games in Chicago and New York in 1939, observed Young, the 32,000 fans in Chicago included only 1,500 whites, and "the white people in New York didn't give a tinker's damn about Negro baseball." Two years later, Young noted, the crowd of 50,000 people who attended the East-West game "didn't have 5,000 white people out."[39]

Although whites rarely attended Negro League games, blacks in many cities frequented major and minor league ballparks. Many African Americans, particularly those who read only mainstream newspapers, were more aware of white baseball than the black alternative. "Scores of people in Harlem . . . do not know there is a colored baseball club in the city," alleged the *Amsterdam News* in 1929. The *Philadelphia Tribune* reported that black children attending a Hilldale game in the 1920s "had heard of Cobb, Speaker, Hornsby and Babe Ruth and other pale-faced stars, but knew that they had players of their own group who could hold their own with any stars of any league." Buck O'Neil recalled that as children in Florida he and his friends, unfamiliar with black baseball, emulated the intensely racist Ty Cobb and other major league players in their imaginary games.[40]

African-American newspapermen repeatedly chided blacks for supporting organized baseball. 'It is bad enough to ride on Jim Crow cars, but to go into ecstasies over a Jim Crow sport is unforgivable," admonished the *Chicago Whip* in 1921. Two years later a sportswriter in Washington DC, where African Americans avidly rooted for the Senators, asked, "Why then should we continue to support, foster and fill the coffers of a national enterprise that has no place or future for men of color, although they have the ability to make the grade?"[41] Wendell Smith offered a scathing critique of black fans in 1938:

Why we continue to flock to major league ball parks, spending our hard earned dough, screaming and hollering, stamping our feet and clapping our hands, begging and pleading for some white batter to knock some white pitcher's ears off, almost having fits if the home team loses and crying for joy when they win, is a question that will probably never be settled satisfactorily. What in the world are we thinking about anyway?

The fact that major league baseball refuses to admit Negro players within its folds makes the question just that much more perplexing. Surely, it's sufficient reason for us to quit spending our money and time in their ball parks. Major league baseball does not want us. It never has. Still we continue to help support this institution that places a bold "Not Welcome" sign over its thriving portal and refuse to patronize the very place that has shown that it is more than welcome to have us. We black folks are a strange tribe![42]

The presence of black fans at white games grated for many reasons. As a Kansas City minister commented about the patronage of white-owned businesses, "All of that money goes into the white man's pocket and then out of our neighborhood." The prevalence of segregated seating provoked additional irritation. In St. Louis, where fans had to sit in a separate area behind a screen, a black newspaper condemned fans who ignored the St. Louis Stars, but chose to "fork over six bits to see a game at Sportsman's Park . . . and get Jim Crowed in the bargain." In Kansas City blacks faced segregated seating at minor league Blues games throughout the 1920s. When former major league catcher Johnny Kling bought the team in the 1930s, he ended this policy, but when the Yankees purchased the club in 1938, the organization reinstituted Jim Crow. Other ballparks, like Griffith Stadium in Washington, had no formal policy dividing the races, but African Americans always sat in specific areas of the outfield. "There were no signs," remembered one black Senators fan. "You just knew that was where you would sit."[43]

Many of these same ballparks regularly hosted Negro League and other black contests. After 50,000 fans attended the all-star extravaganza at Comiskey Park in 1941, Fay Young protested, "The East versus West game ought to make Chicago folk get busy and have a ballyard of their own. Why is it we have to 'rent' the other fellow's belongings?" But the cost of constructing a stadium fell beyond the limited resources of most team owners. Only a handful of teams—the Memphis Red Sox, the Pittsburgh Crawfords in the 1930s, and the Nashville Elite Giants—owned the stadiums they played in.[44] Most leased or rented facilities usually controlled by whites, often in white neighborhoods, and governed by the unpredictable racial mores of the era.

The thorny issue of acquiring a place for black teams to play further illustrated the complex American racial dynamics. For the independent clubs of the early twentieth century, the ability to secure reliable access to a playing field often elevated the team from sandlot to professional level. After 1907 the Indianapolis ABCs held a lease to play at Northwestern Park, a small black-owned stadium in the city's African-American district. The club advertised itself as one of the few black teams to "own their own park" and its ability to guarantee playing dates attracted a steady stream of frontline opponents. In the 1910s Ed Bolden obtained the use of Hilldale Park in Darby, Pennsylvania, just outside Philadelphia. Connected by trolley to

Philadelphia's African-American area, Hilldale Park seated eight thousand fans, providing Bolden's Hilldale Club with a steady following.[45]

Hilldale Park was a curious affair, with several trees and tree stumps scattered through the outfield and a hazardous depression that ran across center field. Indeed, many of the ballparks left much to be desired as playing fields. Early teams in Newark performed at Sprague Stadium, hemmed in on one side by a laundry building so close to the infield that balls hit on its roof became ground-rule doubles. The Baltimore Black Sox played in what the *Afro-American* called "a sewer known as Maryland Park, which featured broken seats, holes in the roof, nonworking toilets and weeds on the field."[46]

As the popularity of black baseball increased, however, teams began renting larger and better white-owned facilities from recreation entrepreneurs or major and minor league teams. Some parks were located in black neighborhoods, but others brought players and fans across town into white districts. When the White Sox abandoned eighteen-thousand-seat South Side Park in Chicago's Black Belt for the new Comiskey Stadium, Charles Comiskey's brother-in-law, John Schorling, refurbished the arena and offered it to Rube Foster's American Giants. After 1923 the Kansas City Monarchs leased Muehlebach Stadium, home of the Kansas City Blues of the American Association, another ballpark located in a black section. The Detroit Stars, on the other hand, played at Mack Park, situated amid a German working-class neighborhood. After Mack Park burned down in 1929 the Stars moved to a field in Hamtramck, a Polish community.[47]

Playing in a white-owned facility raised numerous problems for black teams and players. Many stadiums refused to allow African-American players to use the locker rooms. When the Pittsburgh Crawfords or Homestead Grays played at Ammons Field or Forbes Field, the players had to dress and shower at the local YMCA. Some ballparks, like American Association Park in Kansas City, where the Monarchs played from 1920 to 1922, insisted on segregated seating, even for Negro League games.[48] The shift from a small black-owned arena to a larger white-owned one also raised the specter of racial betrayal. The 1916 move by the ABCs from Northwestern Park to Federal League Park posed a familiar dilemma. Switching to the new park placed the ABCs in a modern facility, comparable to many major league fields. However, as the *Indianapolis Freeman* complained, the relocation would transfer rent and concession money as well as jobs from blacks to whites.[49] When the Lincoln Giants moved their games from Olympic Stadium in Harlem to the more distant, but attractive Protectory Oval, the

New York Amsterdam News protested, "To see a good baseball game in which colored men engage you now have to travel miles out of the district."[50]

By the late 1930s and early 1940s several major and minor league teams had discovered that renting their stadiums for Sunday Negro League doubleheaders could be a lucrative proposition. In 1932 the New York Yankees began scheduling four-team doubleheaders at Yankee Stadium when the Yankees were on the road. In 1939 the Yankees even donated a "Jacob Ruppert Memorial Cup," named after the team's late owner, to the black club that won the most games at the stadium that year. By the end of the decade the Yankees also rented out the ballparks of their Kansas City and Newark affiliates to the Monarchs and Eagles.[51] In 1939 the Baltimore Orioles, who had previously refused to allow the Elite Giants to use Oriole Park, accepted several Sunday dates. The Homestead Grays played regular Sunday dates at Griffith Stadium starting in 1940, averaging better than ten thousand fans a game. Even Shibe Park in Philadelphia, where blacks had rarely played previously, began scheduling Negro League games in the 1940s.[52]

These bookings marked important breakthroughs. They demonstrated the economic potential of black baseball fans and their respectability as well. As the *Kansas City Call* commented in a 1949 editorial, "From a sociological point of view, the Monarchs have done more than any other single agent to break the damnable outrage of prejudice that exists in this city. White fans, the thinking class at least, can not have watched the orderly crowds at Association Park . . . and not concede that we are humans at least, and worthy of consideration as such."[53]

Perhaps the most significant area of racial controversy revolved around the white owners and booking agents who profited from black baseball. In 1917 David Wyatt derided "the white man who has now and in the past secured grounds and induced some one in the role of the 'good old Nigger' to gather a lot of athletes and then used circus methods to drag a bunch of our best citizens out, only to undergo humiliation, with all kinds of indignities flaunted in their faces, while he sits back and grows rich off a percentage of the proceeds."[54] Yet, as Wyatt well knew, few African Americans in the early twentieth century had the resources to underwrite a baseball enterprise. As *Pittsburgh Courier* columnist Rollo Wilson observed in 1933: "Mighty few teams have been entirely financed by Negro capital. . . . There have been many instances of so-called Negro 'owners' being nothing but a 'front' for the white interest behind him."[55] Before the 1930s, when the urban "numbers kings" began bankrolling Negro League franchises, economic survival almost always required either partial or complete white ownership or an alliance with white booking agents who controlled access to playing fields.

Both contemporaries and historians have frequently portrayed white booking agents as the Shylockian villains of black baseball. Operating in a universe in which few African-American teams owned playing fields, these baseball entrepreneurs controlled access to the best ballparks and many of the most popular opponents. Nat Strong personified these individuals. A former sporting goods salesman, Strong, like the men who founded vaudeville, had glimpsed an opportunity to profit along the fringes of American entertainment. Recognizing the broad interest in semiprofessional baseball in the 1890s, Strong gained control of New York–area ball fields like Dexter Park in Queens that hosted these games. He rented out these facilities to white and black teams alike and gradually expanded his empire to include a substantial portion of the East Coast. In 1905 Strong formed the National Association of Colored Professional Clubs of the United States and Cuba, which booked games for the Philadelphia Giants, Cuban X Giants, Brooklyn Royal Giants, and other top eastern black squads.[56]

Any team hoping to schedule lucrative Sunday dates at a profitable site had to deal with Strong, who systematically attempted to secure a monopoly over black professional baseball. Teams that defied Strong found themselves barred from the best bookings. When John Connors, the black owner of the Royal Giants, obtained a playing field in 1911 and attempted to arrange his own games, Strong blacklisted teams that dealt with Connors. Within two years Strong had wrested control of the rebellious franchise from Connors.[57] Black teams also resented the fact that Strong paid a flat guarantee rather than a percentage of the gate, allowing him to reap the profits from large crowds. Behavior like this led former player and organizer Sol White to remark in 1929, "There is not a man in the country who has made as much money from colored ballplaying as Nat Strong, and yet he is the least interested in its welfare."[58]

The creation of the original Negro Leagues in the 1920s occurred against this backdrop. Historians have usually accepted Rube Foster's descriptions of his Negro National League (NNL) as a purer circuit than the rival Eastern Colored League (ECL). Black owners predominated in the NNL; white owners, particularly Strong, prevailed in the ECL. Foster vehemently dismissed the ECL as a tool of Strong. Yet, the reality of the two leagues was more complex.

As Neil Lanctot has demonstrated, the key figure of the ECL was not

Strong, but its president, Ed Bolden. Bolden, a black Philadelphia-area postal worker, had elevated the Hilldale Club of Darby, Pennsylvania, from a sandlot team into a frontline independent competitor. In 1918, when Strong had attempted to gain control of the Hilldale Club, Bolden sent an open letter to the *Philadelphia Tribune*, proclaiming, "The race people of Philadelphia and vicinity are proud to proclaim Hilldale the biggest thing in the baseball world owned, fostered and controlled by race men. . . . To affiliate ourselves with other than race men would be a mark against our name that could never be eradicated."[59] Yet, five years later Bolden allied with Strong to form the ECL. Bolden, heavily dependent on scheduling nonleague games at locales like Dexter Park, owned or controlled by Strong, recognized the benefits of amalgamation. "Close analysis will prove that only where the color line fades and co-operation instituted are our business advances gratified," wrote Bolden in 1925.[60]

If, as Foster and black sportswriters alleged, Strong "was the league and ran the league," his conduct certainly belied this accusation. The ECL failed, in no small measure, because Strong's Brooklyn Royal Giants refused to adhere to the league schedule. A traveling team with no home base, the Royal Giants frequently bypassed the games with league opponents if offered more lucrative bookings. In 1924 the league commissioners voted the Royal Giants out of the ECL, but relented when Strong promised his team would play all scheduled games. His failure to adhere to this pledge greatly weakened the league.[61]

As Bolden noted, however, the Negro National League also had a "few [white] skeletons lurking in the closet."[62] The most visible white presence in the NNL was league secretary J. L. Wilkinson, the owner of the Kansas City Monarchs. Wilkinson represented the best in Negro League ownership, white or black. As Wendell Smith later saluted, he "not only invested his money, but his very heart and soul" in black baseball. But Wilkinson always remained conscious of the need to portray the Monarchs as a black institution. African Americans Dr. Howard Smith and Quincy J. Gilmore became the public faces of the Monarchs, attending league meetings and riding in the lead car at the opening game festivities.[63] In Detroit, first Tenny Blount and later Mose Walker fronted for white businessman John Roesink as owner of the Stars. Most significantly, Foster himself was not the sole owner of the Chicago American Giants. John Schorling, owner of Schorling Stadium, the team's home grounds, underwrote the American Giants and split all profits evenly with Foster. After the *Chicago Broad Ax* protested in 1912 that Schorling received proceeds that "should be received by the Race to whom the patrons of the game belong," Foster concealed Schorling's role. Nonetheless, other NNL owners remained suspicious of Schorling's influence and, when Foster became ill in 1926, Schorling assumed sole ownership of the team.[64]

Nor was the NNL free from the tyranny of booking agents. In this instance, however, the key figure was Foster. As early as 1917 Foster had seized control of scheduling in the Midwest. As president of the NNL, Foster booked all league games and received 5 percent of the gate. Critics leveled charges against Foster's domination similar to those directed at Nat Strong in the East. St. Louis Giants secretary W. S. Ferrance protested Foster's profits noting, "There was not a man connected [with the league] that was not in a position to book his own club and had been doing so for years." Others charged that Foster guaranteed lucrative Sunday home games for his American Giants. One black writer charged that Foster's "race baseball league" was designed to extend his booking agency," just as Foster accused Strong of manipulating the ECL.[65]

Racial controversies also arose in the operations of both leagues, most notably over the issue of employing white umpires. Fay Young protested in 1922, "It isn't necessary for us to sit by the thousands watching eighteen men perform in the national pastime, using every bit of strategy and brain work, to have it all spoiled by thinking it is impossible to have any other man officiating but pale faces."[66] Many owners believed that white arbiters would exercise more authority and better control player rowdiness. They also argued that few blacks had the requisite experience to offer competent officiating. "The colored umpire does not have the advantage that the white umpire has, in passing from sandlot ball to the minor leagues and then to the majors," contended Baltimore Black Sox owner George Rossiter. "As a result of his inexperience he is not able to deliver the goods." Nonetheless, many fans and sportswriters agreed with the verdict of the *Philadelphia Tribune*, which argued, "Regardless of the reason for colored ball games having white umpires it is a disgusting and indefensible practice" and "a reflection on the ability and intelligence of colored people."[67]

The very presence of white owners also continued to rankle many in the African-American community. After a tragic fire injured 219 black fans at Mack Park in Detroit in 1929, some blacks organized a boycott protesting white owner John Roesink's "failure to advertise in 'shine' newspapers, his arrogant, insulting attitude toward patrons of the game" and "his failure to compensate, or visit or even speak kindly to any of the persons injured in the catastrophe at Mack Park." The boycott reportedly "brought Roesink down from his 'high horse'" and elicited a promise that he would stay away from the park and allow his black assistant Mose Walker to operate the Stars.[68]

That same year the *Baltimore Afro-American* attacked the local Black Sox on the umpire issue. Ignoring the fact that both white-owned and black-owned teams employed whites, the *Afro-American* maintained, "If the Sox management were colored, we'd have colored umpires tomorrow."[69]

Both the NNL and ECL collapsed with the onset of the Great Depression. By this time a group of unorthodox, but highly successful, black business-men wealthy enough to finance black professional baseball had arisen in many cities. Cuban Stars' impresario Alessandro (Alex) Pompez pioneered this new breed of owner in the 1920s. Pompez, a Cuban American born in Florida, reigned as the numbers king of Harlem. The numbers game was a poor man's lottery. For as little as a nickel, individuals could gamble on hitting a lucky combination of three numbers and winning a payoff of 600 to 1. Since the true odds of winning were 999 to 1, considerable profits awaited a resourceful and reliable man who could oversee the operation. Pompez reportedly grossed as much as seven to eight thousand dollars a day from his organization. In the 1920s Pompez purchased Dyckman's Oval, a park and stadium in Harlem, and staged a variety of sports events including boxing, wrestling, and motorcycle racing. Pompez, who had strong connections in Cuba and a keen eye for baseball talent, formed the Cuban Stars to play at Dyckman's Oval. In 1923 they joined the ECL, one of only two black-owned clubs in the league. During the 1930s he owned the New York Cubans. Pompez imported top Cuban players like Martin Dihigo and Luis Tiant, Sr., to perform for his teams.[70]

The numbers operations run by Pompez and others were illegal but widely accepted in black America. In a world in which African Americans had few legitimate business opportunities, many of the most talented and resourceful entrepreneurs, men who, according to novelist Richard Wright, "would have been steel tycoons, Wall street brokers, auto moguls had they been white,"[71] entered the numbers racket. Some, like Jim "Soldier Boy" Semler of New York or Dick Kent of St. Louis, were ruthless gangsters, prone to violence and intimidation.[72] Others, like Pompez and Gus Greenlee of Pittsburgh, although not averse to using strong-arm methods to expand and defend their empires, won reputations as community benefactors. Often these numbers kings turned a portion of their profits back into the black community through loans, charity, and investments.[73]

In the 1930s black gambling barons throughout the nation began to follow Pompez into baseball. In Pittsburgh Gus Greenlee, a Pompez friend and protégé whose peak income has been estimated at $20,000 to $25,000 a day, launched the Pittsburgh Crawfords. In Detroit Everett Wilson, numbers partner of John Roxborough who managed Joe Louis, bought the

Detroit Stars from John Roesink. Abe Manley, a retired numbers banker from Camden, owned first the Brooklyn and then the Newark Eagles. Semler ran the New York Black Yankees and Rufus "Sonnyman" Jackson supplied needed capital for Cum Posey's Homestead Grays. When Greenlee united the eastern teams into a new Negro National League in 1933, league meetings, according to Donn Rogosin, brought together "the most powerful black gangsters in the nation."[74]

Their wealth, power, and influence within the black community notwithstanding, the numbers kings still had to make their way in a white-dominated world. Of the Negro National League teams of the 1930s and 1940s, only the Pittsburgh Crawfords owned and operated their own stadium. All teams still relied heavily on white booking agents for scheduling. Nat Strong had died in the early 1930s, but William Leuchsner who ran Nat C. Strong Baseball Enterprises in the New York area, and Eddie Gottlieb, who operated out of Philadelphia, now ruled Strong's domain.[75] In the Midwest, where a new Negro American League formed in 1937, Abe Saperstein, better known as the founder of the Harlem Globetrotters, had succeeded Rube Foster as the preeminent booking agent. Saperstein even received 5 percent of the substantial gate at the East-West showcase.[76] These arrangements were not without benefits for Negro League teams. Gottlieb, for example, coordinated ticket sales and newspaper and poster publicity for events he booked, enabling teams to reduce their overhead and maintain fewer employees. The booking agents also negotiated reduced rental, operating, and insurance fees from major and minor league ballparks. The Homestead Grays reported that Gottlieb's intervention with the New York Yankees saved league owners ten thousand dollars in 1940.[77]

Nonetheless, many owners bridled at the influence of white booking agents and repeatedly sought to be free of them. According to Effa Manley, who owned the Newark Eagles with her husband, Abe, "[We] fought a . . . war against the booking agents from the first day [we] entered the picture . . . but [we] fought a losing battle. The tentacle-like grip of the booking agents proved impossible to break." Their resistance cost the Eagles their Yankee Stadium playing dates in 1939 and 1940. At the 1940 league meetings, the Manleys demanded the removal of Gottlieb as booking agent for Yankee Stadium. According to *Baltimore Afro-American* sports editor Art Carter, Effa Manley "assumed the position that the league was a colored organization and that she wanted to see all the money kept within the group." When Posey defended Gottlieb, Manley (who, although she lived as a black woman, later claimed to be white) denounced the Grays' owner as a "handkerchief head," a street-slang variation on "Uncle Tom."[78] That same year black sportswriters at the East-West game organized the American Sportswriters Association to protest Saperstein's domination of that event and the Negro American League removed Saperstein as its official booking agent. The fact that Strong, Leuchsner, Gottlieb, and Saperstein were all Jewish injected elements of anti-Semitism into these disputes.[79]

The race issue also reared its head in hiring decisions. On several occasions teams hired whites to handle publicity in hopes that they might be able to better attract more whites to the games, much to the chagrin of black sportswriters. In the 1920s, when Ed Bolden hired a local white sportswriter as the ECL umpire supervisor to garner attention, John Howe of the *Philadelphia Tribune* called it inappropriate to hire whites in a league "of . . . for . . . and by Negroes." Greenlee employed Saperstein to publicize the East-West game in the 1930s, but the move brought out few white fans.[80] Even the Manleys, who demanded black control, had, in the words of sportswriter Ed Harris, "the temerity to hire a white press agent to do their work," evoking widespread criticism. One columnist noted, "Speaking of unholy alliances, how about the one between . . . the Negro owner of a Negro baseball team who hires a white press agent." Oliver "Butts" Brown of the *New Jersey Herald News*, protested: "No white publicity man could be of much assistance to you in the many things you hope to do to improve the condition of Negro baseball. In fact he would be a detriment."[81]

These conflicts and debates over the role of whites in black baseball revealed not just the racial tensions that always existed in the age of segregation, but the stake of African Americans in successful black-owned and -operated institutions. "Who owns the Grays?" reflected the *Washington Afro-American* in 1943. "It is a pleasure to inform the fans of Washington that the Washington Homestead Grays are owned and operated by three colored gentleman."[82] A scene at the opening game of the 1946 Negro League World Series captured this sense of pride. When heavyweight champion Joe Louis threw out the first pitch, he tossed a silver ball that had been awarded to the Cuban Giants, the first great black professional team, for winning a tournament in 1888. As James Overmyer writes, "With a sweep of his right arm, Louis, the greatest black athlete of his day, symbolically linked the earliest era of Negro baseball with its most recent high point."[83]

The World Series ceremony occurred at a critical juncture in the history of black baseball. In September 1946 Jackie Robinson was completing his successful first season in organized baseball. The response to Robinson revealed the fragile hold that all-black baseball held on the African-American psyche. From its earliest days, the promoters of the African-American game had made its transitional nature clear. In *The History of Colored Baseball* in

1906, Sol White advised the black ballplayer to take the game "seriously . . . as honest efforts with his great ability will open an avenue in the near future wherein he might walk hand-in-hand with the opposite race in the greatest of all American games." In a remarkably prescient passage, White added, "There are grounds for hoping that some day the bar will drop and some good man will be chosen out of the colored profession that will be a credit to all, and pave the way for others to follow."[84] Rube Foster had another vision, wherein an all-black team would pierce the ranks of the white professional leagues, but the model of ultimate integration remained. *The Crisis*, the journal of the National Association for the Advancement of Colored People, left no doubt as to the ultimate purpose of the Negro Leagues. "It is only through the elevation of our Negro league baseball that colored ballplayers will break into white major league ball," avowed *The Crisis* in 1938. Even as strong an advocate of "race baseball" as Fay Young who railed against white umpires, publicity men, and booking agents, joined the chorus. "We want Negroes in the major leagues if they have to crawl to get there," wrote Young in 1945.[85]

Most people involved with black baseball had few illusions as to what the impact of integration would be. Asked about the prospect of blacks in the major leagues in 1939, Homestead Grays manager Vic Harris replied, "If they start picking them up, what are the remaining players going to do to make a living? . . . And suppose our stars—the fellows who do draw well—are gobbled up by the big clubs. How could the other 75 or 80 percent survive?" Black sportswriters like Sam Lacy "knew [that integration] would have a devastating effect on black baseball."[86] Joe Bostic wrote in 1942:

> Today, there are two Negro organized leagues, just on the threshold of emergence as real financial factors. . . . To kill [them] would be criminal and that's just what the entry of their players into the American and National Leagues would do.
>
> Nor should money from the byproducts be overlooked such as the printers, the Negro papers and the other advertising media, which get their taste: the officials, scorekeepers, announcers, secretaries and a host of others. These monies are coming into Negro pockets. You can rest assured that we'd get none of those jobs in the other leagues, *even with a player or two in their leagues*.
>
> In sum: From an idealist and democratic point of view, we say "yes" to Negroes in the two other leagues. From the point of practicality: "No."[87]

But for Lacy, Bostic, and others, "the idealistic and democratic point of view" won out. Less than three years after issuing his admonition, Bostic ardently pursued the policy he had condemned, confronting Branch Rickey with Negro League players Terris McDuffie and Dave Thomas and demanding a tryout with the Dodgers during spring training in 1945. Wendell Smith might criticize black fans for attending white games, but, working alongside Rickey, he became one of the key architects of baseball integration. Sam Lacy acknowledged, "After Jackie, the Negro Leagues [became] a symbol I couldn't live with anymore." For these sportswriters, as James Overmyer points out, "covering baseball integration [was] the biggest story of their lives" and they pursued it wholeheartedly.[88]

Throughout black America the focus shifted from the Negro Leagues to the major leagues. The African-American press reduced its coverage of the Negro Leagues to make room for updates and statistics about Robinson and other black players in organized baseball. Advertisements appeared for special rail excursions to National League cities to see Robinson play. Even the Negro Leagues themselves attempted to capitalize on Robinson's popularity. The cover of the 1946 Negro League yearbook featured Robinson rather than one of the established league stars. A program for the Philadelphia Stars in the late 1940s pictured Robinson in his Dodger uniform.[89]

Negro League fans voted with their dollars decisively in favor of integration. In 1946 Effa Manley found that "our fans would go as far as Baltimore" to see Robinson play for the Montreal Royals.[90] Once he joined the Dodgers and New York–area fans could see Robinson in eighty-eight games at Ebbets Field and the Polo Grounds, attendance plummeted for the Newark Eagles and New York Black Yankees. Other teams also felt the pinch. "People wanted to go to see the Brooklynites," recalled Monarch pitcher Hilton Smith. "Even if we were playing here in Kansas City, people wanted to go over to St. Louis to see Jackie."[91]

Occasionally critics raised their voices to protest the abandonment of black baseball. "Around 400 players are involved in the Negro version of the national pastime," warned Dan Burley in *The Amsterdam News* in 1948. "If there are no customers out to see them, they don't earn a living. In enriching the coffers of the major league clubs, we put the cart before the horse for no purpose."[92] But most commentators were less sympathetic. In response to Manley's complaints about declining fan support, the *Kansas City Call* cajoled, "The day of loyalty to Jim Crow anything is fast passing away. Sister, haven't you heard the news? Democracy is a-coming fast."[93] The Manleys sold the Eagles after the 1948 season. By the early 1950s all but a handful of the Negro League clubs had disbanded.

As Burley, Manley, and others had predicted, the end of segregation would mean that fewer, rather than more, African Americans would earn their living from baseball in the latter half of the twentieth century. The failure of major league teams to hire black managers, coaches, and front-office personnel compounded this problem. The nearly universal celebration of Jackie Robinson's triumph notwithstanding, integration would produce negative as well as positive consequences.

Cultural critic Gerald Early sees the demise of the Negro Leagues as the destruction of "an important black economic and cultural institution" that encompassed many of the best and worst elements of African-American life. Blacks, writes Early, "have never gotten over the loss of the Negro Leagues because they have never completely understood the ironically compressed expression of shame and pride, of degradation and achievement that those leagues represented."[94] In the final analysis, the black baseball experience captured the "twoness" in the "souls of black folk" as well as the "dogged strength" that kept them "from being torn asunder."

NOTES

1. On Rube Foster, see Robert Peterson, *Only the Ball Was White: A History of the Legendary Black Players and All-Black Professional Teams* (Englewood Cliffs: Prentice-Hall, 1970), 103–15; Donn Rogosin, *Invisible Men: Life in Baseball's Negro Leagues* (New York: Atheneum, 1983), 33; Janet Bruce, *The Kansas City Monarchs: Champions of Black Baseball* (Lawrence: University Press of Kansas, 1985), 31–32; Neil Lanctot, *Fair Dealing and Clean Playing: The Hilldale Club and the Development of Black Professional Baseball, 1910–1932* (Jefferson NC: McFarland, 1994), 29; and Jules Tygiel, "Black Ball" in John Thorn, Pete Palmer, Michael Gershman, and David Pietrusza, *Total Baseball*, 5th ed. (New York: Viking, 1991), 435.

2. The literature on black baseball is extraordinarily rich. The pioneering works in this field include Peterson, *Only the Ball Was White*, and Donn Rogosin, *Invisible Men*. An impressive body of team and community studies has supplemented these overviews. This chapter relies heavily on Richard Bak, *Turkey Stearnes and His Detroit Stars: The Negro Leagues in Detroit, 1919–1933* (Detroit: Wayne State University Press, 1994); Janet Bruce, *The Kansas City Monarchs*; Paul Debono, *The Indianapolis ABCs: History of a Premier Team in the Negro Leagues* (Jefferson NC: McFarland, 1997); Neil Lanctot, *Fair Dealing and Clean Playing*; James Overmyer, *Effa Manley and the Newark Eagles* (Metuchen NY: Scarecrow Press, 1993); and Rob Ruck, *Sandlot Seasons: Sport in Black Pittsburgh* (Urbana: University of Illinois Press, 1987). Two photographic histories of black baseball, Bruce Chadwick, *When*

the Game Was Black and White: The Illustrated History of the Negro Leagues (New York: Abbeville Press, 1992), and Phil Dixon, with Patrick J. Hannigan, *The Negro Baseball Leagues: A Photographic History* (New York: Amereon House, 1992), were also very helpful as was Jim Reisler, *Black Writers/Black Baseball: An Anthology of Articles from Black Sportswriters Who Covered the Negro Leagues* (Jefferson NC: McFarland, 1994). For those interested in learning more about the stars of black baseball, the oral histories of John Holway and the reference works of James A. Riley are indispensable.

3. W. E. B. DuBois, *Souls of Black Folk* (New York: Vintage Books/Library of America, 1990).

4. Overmyer, 111; Lanctot, 23; Bruce, 44.

5. Bruce, 42, 49.

6. Bak, 135.

7. James H. Bready, *Baseball in Baltimore* (Baltimore: The Johns Hopkins University Press, 1998), 174; Lanctot, 61; Bruce, 45–47.

8. Rogosin, 32–33; Reisler, 49.

9. Debono, 2, 44–48.

10. Lanctot, 23.

11. On the Negro National League, see Debono, 49, 84; Bak, 71.

12. Bruce, 88; Reisler, 60.

13. Lanctot, 66; Bruce, 24, 45; Overmyer, 266.

14. Debono, 101.

15. Overmyer, 15–17, 59, 215.

16. Overmyer, 5, 59–60, 167–68, 174; Bruce, 45; Lanctot, 176.

17. Debono, 74; Steven J. Ross, *Black Diamonds, Blues City* (film); Overmyer, 86.

18. Bak, 183; James Bankes, *The Pittsburgh Crawfords: The Life and Times of Baseball's Most Exciting Team* (Dubuque IA: Wm. C. Brown, 1991).

19. James M. DiClerico and Barry Pavelec, *The Jersey Game: The History of Modern Baseball from Its Birth to the Big Leagues in the Garden State* (New Brunswick NJ: Rutgers University Press, 1991), 146.

20. Imamu Amiri Baraka, *The Autobiography of LeRoi Jones/Amiri Baraka* (New York: Freundlich Books, 1984), 35.

21. Bak, 126; Bready, 166; Bruce, 42.

22. Baraka, 35; Overmyer, 66.

23. Bankes, 104–5; Ross, *Black Diamonds*; Chadwick, 54; Overmyer, 112; Bruce, 44.

24. Bruce, 3.

25. Debono, 73.

26. Bruce, 44–45.

27. Chadwick, 50; Debono, 180.

28. Overmyer, 34, 64, 97; Reisler, 99–100; Ruck, 157; Bready, 181; Bruce, 47.

29. Bak, 87; Ross, *Black Diamonds*; Overmyer, 63.

30. Overmyer, 63.

31. Brad Snyder, Senior Thesis, Duke University, 1994.

32. Chadwick, 55; Peterson, 113; Ross, *Black Diamonds*.

33. Bruce, 58.

34. Charles E. Whitehead, *A Man and His Diamonds: A Story of the Great Andrew (Rube) Foster, the Outstanding Team He Owned and Managed and the Superb League He Founded and Commissioned* (New York: Vantage Press, 1980), 180.

35. Lanctot, 112–20; Overmyer, 107.

36. Lanctot, 40, 62–63.

37. Lanctot, 121; Overmyer, 113–14.

38. Debono, 22, 42; Lanctot, 62; Bruce, 44–45.

39. Overmyer, 166; Reisler, 60, 61.

40. Lanctot, 184; Ross, *Black Diamonds*.

41. Lanctot, 183–84.

42. Reisler, 36–37.

43. Bruce, 29, 51–52; Lanctot, 184; Snyder, 4.

44. Reisler, 61; Dixon and Hannigan, 176.

45. Debono, 20; Lanctot, 20, 23.

46. Lanctot, 60; Overmyer, 104–5; Bready, 167.

47. Lanctot, 37; Bruce, 52–53; Bak, 57, 186.

48. Bankes, 25; Bruce, 51.

49. Debono, 66–67.

50. Lanctot, 99.

51. Overmyer, 122.

52. Bready, 175; Snyder, 2–9; Bruce Kuklick, *To Every Thing a Season: Shibe Park and Urban Philadelphia, 1909–1976* (Princeton NJ: Princeton University Press, 1991), 146–47.

53. Chadwick, 121.

54. Bruce, 11.

55. Ruck, 116.

56. On Nat Strong, see Lanctot, 29, 62.

57. Lanctot, 29.

58. Overmyer, 269.

59. Lanctot, 73–74.

60. Lanctot, 66.

61. Bruce, 31; Lanctot, 145, 162.

62. Lanctot, 96.

63. Ruck, 221; Bruce, 21–22.

64. Bak, 55–57, 202; Lanctot, 37–38; Peterson, 113–14.

65. Dixon, 99; Ruck, 123; Peterson, 113.

66. Bruce, 29.

67. Lanctot, 198–200.

68. Bak, 186–87, 192.

69. Lanctot, 200.

70. Overmyer, 10, 272–77; Bankes, 91–92.

71. Rogosin, 104.

72. Bankes, 94.

73. Overmyer, 9–10; Ruck, 149–50.

74. Rogosin, 107.

75. Overmyer, 268–69.

76. Bruce, 90.

77. Overmyer, 135, 139.

78. Overmyer, 134, 138–39.

79. Bruce, 90; Lanctot, 95.

80. Lanctot, 132; Bankes, 115.

81. Overmyer, 113–14, 140.

82. Snyder, 2–24.

83. Overmyer, 204.

84. Dixon, 241–42; Peterson, 59.

85. Dixon, 242; H. B. Webber and Oliver Brown, "Play Ball!" *Crisis* 45 (May 1938), 137; Bruce, 111.

86. Reisler, 13, 16.

87. Reisler, 80–81.

88. Reisler, 13; Overmyer, 244.

89. Overmyer, 108–9; Debono, 121; Chadwick, 165; Dixon, 252.

90. Overmyer, 235.

91. Bruce, 116.

92. Reisler, 143.

93. Bruce, 116.

94. Geoffrey C. Ward and Ken Burns, *Baseball: An Illustrated History* (New York: Alfred A. Knopf, 1994), 413.

SEVEN

Introduction to *It's Good to Be Alive*

In April 1958 the transplanted Brooklyn Dodgers confronted the Los Angeles Coliseum, their new home field, for the first time. The remodeled football stadium never was meant to host major league baseball. Left field measured only 250 feet from home plate and club officials had constructed an artificial ninety-foot "China Wall" to better challenge hitters. Pitcher Carl Erskine saw the fence and immediately thought of his longtime batterymate. "Son of a buck," he mused. "If Campy was well, he'd break Ruth's record, popping flies over that dinky screen."

But Roy Campanella, arguably the greatest catcher to play the game, was not well. Two months earlier a rented car he was driving had skidded on a patch of ice, smashed into a Long Island lamp post, and overturned, leaving Campanella trapped inside with a broken neck. As Erskine and the Dodgers prepared for a new season, strangers on a strange field, Campanella lay paralyzed, never to walk, much less play, again.

Carl Erskine was not the only one to ponder the saddest words "what might have been" with regard to Roy Campanella. His major league life, foreshortened at its outset by racial discrimination, had now been prematurely ended by tragedy. Indeed Campanella's entire career, glorious enough to merit his eventual first-ballot election to the Baseball Hall of Fame, raises echoes of blocked possibilities and unfulfilled promises. If not for baseball's color barrier, Campanella might have entered the major leagues a half-decade or more earlier, compiling records that catchers would still strive to break; if not for the politics of integration, he, and not Jackie Robinson, might have been the first black player; and if not for his crippling accident, Campanella may well have become major league baseball's first black manager, saving the game from one of its long-standing embarrassments.

Roy Campanella was born in 1921, the son of an Italian-American father and an African-American mother. His Philadelphia childhood introduced him to a world of racial contradictions: his playmates, both white and black, called him "half-breed"; his father found it "too embarrassing" to attend the family's all-black Baptist church; Campy played, at times, for black sandlot teams against white opponents and, at other times, as the only African American on all-white teams.

So prodigious were Campanella's talents that at age fifteen he found himself catching for the Baltimore Elite (pronounced E-Light) Giants, one of the great Negro League teams of the Depression and World War II era. With the Elite Giants Campanella had the good fortune to fall under the guidance of player-manager Biz Mackey, who, if justice prevails, will someday join his protégé in the Hall of Fame. Campanella called Josh Gibson the greatest Negro League catcher, but many of their playing contemporaries gave Mackey the nod, as did black fans, who, in a 1952 Pittsburgh Courier poll named Mackey the top receiver in Negro League history. "Nobody ever had a better teacher," praised Campy. From Mackey, Campanella learned the rudiments of the catching trade that would distinguish Campanella's career: handling pitchers, blocking low pitches, and the quick-release "snap-throw" from behind the plate.

Unlike Jackie Robinson, who found his brief stint in the Negro Leagues degrading and distasteful, Campanella valued his years in black baseball equally with those in the integrated game. In summarizing his baseball life, Campanella wrote, "I completed exactly twenty years in organized professional baseball, ten years in Negro ball and ten in the National League." Fittingly, in *It's Good to Be Alive*, he devotes roughly equal space to the two phases of his career.

Even after two decades of intense interest and research in Negro League baseball, Campanella's 1960 reminiscences remain one of the most vibrant and perceptive accounts of this lost era. He describes a world in which "anything went . . . spitballs, shine balls, emery balls. . . . I was never sure what the ball would do once it left the pitcher's hand." In the winter months, Campanella and other Negro Leaguers played in the Caribbean, extending his season to fifty weeks a year. Nonetheless, he concluded, "A Negro ballplayer, playing Negro ball in the United States might not have lived like a king, but he didn't live bad either."

But if Campanella accepted, enjoyed, and always spoke fondly of his life in Jim Crow baseball, his ambivalence about the Negro Leagues speaks volumes about racial attitudes in post–World War II America. Recent historians have tended to romanticize the Negro League experience, but those who played the game always remained painfully aware that they had been relegated to a second-rate existence. The urge to compete in the white major leagues remained strong. Campanella may have believed, as he writes, that "the big leagues were as far away as Siberia," but he never hesitated when offered the opportunity to embark on that chilly, difficult journey. He signed on with an abortive *Daily Worker* tryout effort with the Pittsburgh Pirates and offered his services to the Philadelphia Phillies. Although an established star in the Negro Leagues and one of the better paid black players, Campanella did not hesitate when offered a $185 a month salary to play in a Class B minor league.

Indeed, contrary to the legend that portrays Jackie Robinson as the only man who could have withstood the rigors of baseball's "great experiment," Campanella could just as easily have become the focal point of baseball integration. In 1945, when Brooklyn Dodger president Branch Rickey dispatched his scouts to comb the United States and Caribbean for African-American talent, they reached a quick consensus on the stocky catcher. "We were all in on scouting Campanella," recalled Dodger scout Clyde Sukeforth. "You couldn't go wrong there." Rickey considered naming Campanella as his standard-bearer, and at one time planned to announce the signing of Robinson and Campanella simultaneously.

Campanella projected a different persona than Robinson. Equally competitive but far less combative, Campy always took a more conciliatory stance than Robinson. He attributed his differences from Robinson to the unusual demands of the position he played. "I thought of myself as a catcher first, not as a Negro," he explained. "A catcher has to make people like him, no matter what.... I had to make everyone work with me.... You can't be demanding. You have to have a piece of sugar in your hand." But the philosophical gulf that existed between the two Dodger stars was far more significant and profound than Campanella admitted. Robinson, always keenly aware of his status and responsibility as "the first," often sought out confrontation and never avoided controversy. He viewed his triumph as a stepping stone for future progress. Campanella, on the other hand, preached patience, not militancy. When Branch Rickey asked him to delay his major league career so that he might integrate the American Association, Campanella responded, "I'm a ballplayer, not a pioneer." In assessing the slow progress of civil rights, Campy, ignoring one of the most obvious lessons of the Robinson saga, could proclaim, "I'm willing to wait. All this came by waiting."

If, however, Campanella did not possess Robinson's crusading charisma, there can be little doubt that he would have gotten the job done. "Roy was a calm man," says his longtime friend and teammate Don Newcombe,

"He could withstand that kind of pressure. He was just dogged enough to really stick with it." While Robinson performed his heroics in the broad spotlight of Brooklyn, Campanella, although already a ten-year veteran of professional baseball, blazed a quieter but equally effective trail in the minor leagues. In 1946 he starred at Nashua in the Class-B New England League; in 1947 he jumped to the top Dodger farm club at Montreal. "Campanella is the best catcher in the business—major or minor leagues," declared manager Paul Richards. "If (Rickey) doesn't bring that guy up, he may as well go out of the emancipation business." In the locker rooms, Campanella, his hand full of sugar, participated in the traditional teasing and banter, influencing teammates and winning friends. "These were the same things that were missing in the same room last year," commented sportswriter Sam Maltin, comparing the respective stints of Campanella and Robinson at Montreal.

When Roy Campanella finally reached the major leagues for good in July 1948, he celebrated with nine hits, including two home runs and a triple, in his first three games. Over the next ten seasons, despite recurrent injuries, he won three Most Valuable Player Awards and helped to lead the Brooklyn Dodgers to five pennants and a World Championship. In 1953 he established records for home runs (42), RBIS (142), and putouts for a catcher. Baseball historian Bill James asserts, "If Roy Campanella had been healthy three or four more years, there would be no dispute about who was the greatest catcher of all time."

The events of the early morning hours of January 28, 1958, however, brought a premature close to Campy's career. The accident that almost took his life snapped his neck and left him paralyzed from the chest down. It ended not only his days as a player, but also his hopes of full-time coaching or managing in the major leagues. Of the first generation of black major leaguers, Campanella seemed the most likely to be offered the opportunity to guide a team. Baseball executives have a penchant for selecting former catchers to manage; many of Campanella's catching contemporaries, including his New York counterparts Yogi Berra and Wes Westrum, ultimately directed teams. In this selection, his more stolid, pleasing personality would have given him an advantage over the more tempestuous Robinson.

From early in his career, Campanella had been tapped as having managerial potential. He had served as a player-manager in Venezuelan winter ball, and at Nashua in the New England League, Walter Alston had appointed him his assistant manager. When Alston was ejected from a game, Campanella had guided the team to a come-from-behind victory, sending pitcher Don Newcombe up to pinch-hit a game-winning home run. Both Branch Rickey and later Dodger owner Walter O'Malley had approached Campanella about coaching or managing when his playing career had ended. "You mean you're wondering how it would be for you, a Negro, coaching white players?" Campanella quotes O'Malley as saying in 1953. "I don't think you need worry about that. No, I see no problem in you being the first Negro coach." But these dreams were dashed on the Long Island ice. Almost two decades would pass before baseball would deign to hire a black manager, and few people in the 1960s and 1970s would consider the prospect of a man in a wheelchair piloting a major league team.

Roy Campanella's autobiography is, however, not solely, or even primarily, a book about baseball. *It's Good to Be Alive*, written less than eighteen months after the accident, marked Campanella's acceptance of a new role. Suddenly, Campanella, once one of the nation's most celebrated athletes, had become its most famous quadriplegic. "All of my life I have fought, in my own way, for equality and understanding of minority groups," he wrote, "But from here on, I've taken on an even bigger job—fighting for the equality, integration and understanding and acceptance of the severely handicapped."

Campanella would fight this battle, as he had his first, "in (his) own way." In the struggle for racial integration, he had sought to persuade by example and good will. He pursued the same strategy in his new crusade. Later disability rights advocates would, like Jackie Robinson, demand that society acknowledge and correct the obstacles that precluded them from full participation in life. Campanella would be patient, believing that his example would bring acceptance and change.

In both its title and tone, the message of *It's Good to Be Alive* is unmistakable. "I'm a lucky guy. I've got so much to be thankful for. Don't feel sorry for me," insisted Campy. "Even when I had the accident I was lucky. How many people have similar accidents and are killed?" Through faith, acceptance, and hard work, those afflicted by hardship could not just survive, but triumph. "I don't think the Lord has turned his back on me," preached Campanella. "This was a little tough break that had happened to me. But it was something I could handle with the help of the Good Lord."

Campanella's profound faith and bouyant optimism suffuses his autobiography. But Campanella also presented, for the first time for many readers, a graphic account of the psychological pain and demanding physical regimen of the quadriplegic. He recalled his shock on learning of his condition: "I didn't want to be part of the world. I . . . hope that it would remember me as I was—as a ballplayer—not like this." He described arduous therapy sessions where he had to learn to sit up, then feed himself, and, ironically, to catch a ball: "It didn't hit me at first. I didn't get the full meaning at once. But then it came through to me . . . She was gonna teach me—Roy Campanella—how to catch a ball."

Campanella's account of his return to the ballpark for a 1958 World Series game at Yankee Stadium captures the embarrassment and anxiety of the quadriplegic. Because his wheelchair couldn't fit through the aisle, Campy was lifted and carried. "I felt like some sad freak," he recalled. "It was the most embarrassing thing that ever happened to me. I felt ashamed. It was awful." When fans began to cheer, Campy thought " 'I don't want that!' But what could I do? I couldn't get up and leave." Once seated, Campanella faced a new wave of concerns: "I was worried whether I could sit in the seat without a belt or some other means of support. When you're paralyzed you worry about everything that's new." Characteristically, Campanella drew from this experience a lesson of hope: "I accepted the cheers in my heart. Just like they were meant . . . and Lord how they helped." The idea that stadiums might be made more accessible to those in wheelchairs would await the next generation of advocates.

It's Good to Be Alive concludes, as it begins, with a tone of inspirational uplift, a tale of an individual and his family surviving tragedy and adjusting to a challenging new reality. Quadriplegics, Campy had proven, could make contributions to society and live fulfilling lives. "I've always enjoyed life and I'm going to continue to enjoy life even if I have to do it in a wheelchair for the rest of my life," Campanella promised his fans. There were indications that the Campanellas might soon follow the Dodgers to California's promised land.

But Campanella's travails had not yet ended. Ruthe Campanella, portrayed here as the most devoted of wives, did not adjust easily to life with a quadriplegic. By August 1960, Roy, still living in New York, sued Ruthe for legal separation, citing instances of drinking, infidelity, and physical abuse. Campanella withdrew his suit, but the marriage continued to struggle until on January 26, 1963, almost exactly five years from the date of Campy's car crash, Ruthe Campanella died suddenly of a cerebral hemorrhage.

Even this additional tragedy could not shatter Campanella's evanescent spirit or alter his philosophy of life. The year after Ruthe's death, Campanella married his neighbor, Roxie Doles. And, as Campy liked to say, Roxie, together with the Dodgers, "helped me put my life back together." Throughout the remainder of the 1960s Campanella continued to operate his Harlem liquor store, conducted baseball clinics for inner-city youth, and became a familiar figure on New York radio and television programs. Dodger president Walter O'Malley had promised Campanella that he would always have a place in the Dodger family, and each spring, Campy traveled to Dodgertown at Vero Beach, where he worked with young catchers and other Dodger hopefuls. In 1969, Campy won election to the Baseball Hall of Fame. By the early 1970s, when Roger Kahn, preparing his classic volume, *The Boys of Summer*, visited Campanella, he found the old catcher emotionally, if not physically, recovered from his ordeal. Kahn marveled "at the vaunting human spirit, in the noble wreckage of the athlete, in the dazzling palace of the man."

In 1978 Peter O'Malley, Walter's son, who had taken over the Dodger presidency, asked Campanella to move to Los Angeles to work in the club's community services department. Campy sold his liquor store and, finally, twenty years after the Dodgers had moved west, he and Roxie joined them in California. A popular and inspirational public speaker, Campanella became active in local community and volunteer work. He was a fixture at Dodger Stadium, where, health permitting, he rarely missed a game. He continued his annual odyssey to Vero Beach, where Campy's Corner, the outdoor area where Roy held court, became a gathering place for players, coaches, newsmen, and fans. They listened raptly to Campanella's tales, frequently punctuated by his loud cackling laugh, of life in the Negro, minor and major leagues. Several generations of Dodger catchers from John Roseboro through Mike Piazza benefited from his counsel. In the 1980s he recreated this role at Dodger fantasy camps where, recalls former teammate Duke Snider, "We'd have a ball. . . . He was about the most positive person I've been around."

Throughout these years, Campanella continued to experience physical problems resulting from his injuries and paralysis, necessitating many operations and hospital stays. He nonetheless retained his optimism and exuberance. "I'm having a wonderful second life," he told a reporter, echoing the message he had conveyed in *It's Good to Be Alive*. "I want to tell everyone about it. I want them to remember that when trouble comes, it isn't always bad. Take it with a smile, do the best you can and the good Lord will help you out."

On June 27, 1993, Campanella's intrepid heart finally wore down. He had lived almost half of his seventy-one years as a quadriplegic. Peter O'Malley hailed him as "the greatest Dodger of them all." But by this time, Roy Campanella had transcended both the team and the game that had first brought him fame. Born the member of one embattled minority, he had, through his efforts and example, helped to transform the nation's consciousness and usher in an age of new possibilities in race relations.

At midlife, he became a member of yet another embattled minority, and once again served as an inspiration, awakening people to the plight, and more importantly, the potential of the disabled. If we can never know what Roy Campanella's life "might have been," we may nonetheless revel in the marvelous life he created.

EIGHT

Black Ball

The Integrated Game

When slowly and grudgingly given their chance in the years after 1947, blacks conclusively proved their competitive abilities on the diamond, but discrimination persisted as baseball executives continued to deny them the opportunity to display their talents in managerial and front office positions.

Branch Rickey's initiative in breaking the color barrier and Jackie Robinson's dramatic success with the Montreal Expos in 1946 and the Brooklyn Dodgers in 1947 failed to inspire many other team owners to sign African-American ballplayers. In August 1946 major league executives debated a controversial report discussing the "race question," which argued that integration would "lessen the value of several major league franchises." No other clubs moved to sign black players. Only four blacks, all in the Brooklyn system, joined Robinson in organized baseball in 1946. At Nashua, New Hampshire, in the New England League, the Dodger farm club fielded catcher Roy Campanella and pitcher Don Newcombe. The Nashua Dodgers won the league championship largely due to Campanella's hitting and Newcombe's hurling. In the small town of Trois-Rivières in Quebec, pitchers John Wright and Roy Partlow, both of whom had appeared briefly with Robinson at Montreal, led a third Dodger farm team to the Canadian-American league crown. Nonetheless, at the start of the 1947 season, no additional black players appeared on major or minor league rosters.

Robinson's success on the field with the Dodgers and at the box office in 1947 finally stimulated some movement on the part of other clubs to hire black players. In Cleveland Bill Veeck recruited twenty-three-year-old Larry Doby, who went straight from the Negro League Newark Eagles to the Indians in July. Used sparingly, Doby batted a meager .156, casting doubts upon his future. The St. Louis Browns, seeking to boost flagging attendance, signed Willard Brown and Hank Thompson of the Kansas City Monarchs. When the turnstiles failed to respond, the Browns released both

Brown and Thompson, although the latter had established himself as a top prospect. In the National League, the Dodgers signed Dan Bankhead to bolster the club's pitching down the stretch. On August 25, Bankhead, the first black pitcher to appear in the major leagues, surrendered eight runs in three innings but also slammed a home run in his initial at bat.

In addition to the five athletes who appeared in the major leagues, a handful of blacks surfaced in the minors. Campanella succeeded Robinson at Montreal. Newcombe returned to Nashua where he won nineteen games. The independent Stamford Bombers of the Colonial League fielded six black players, and two blacks, including future major leaguer Chuck Harmon, played in the Canadian-American League. Veteran Negro League hurler Nate Moreland won twenty games in California's Class C Sunset League. For the most part, however, organized baseball continued to ignore the treasure trove of black talent submerged in the Negro Leagues. A full year would pass before additional major league teams would add black players to their chains.

In 1948 the integration focus shifted from the Dodgers, where Robinson now reigned at second base, to the Cleveland Indians. In spring training, Larry Doby, who had performed so dismally in 1947, unexpectedly won a starting berth in the Cleveland outfield. After an erratic early season stretch in which Doby alternated errors and strikeouts with tape-measure home runs, he batted .301 and became a key performer for the American League champion Indians. In July Cleveland owner Bill Veeck added the legendary Satchel Paige to the team. Amidst charges that his signing had been a publicity stunt, the forty-two-year-old Paige won six out of seven decisions, including back-to-back shutouts, and posted a 2.47 earned run average. Standing-room-only crowds greeted him in Washington, Chicago, Boston, and even in Cleveland's mammoth Municipal Stadium. The Indians, after defeating the Boston Red Sox in a pennant playoff, won the World Series in six games with Doby's .318 average leading the club.

In 1947 the Dodgers had integrated and reached the World Series; in 1948 the Indians had duplicated and surpassed this achievement. Both teams had set all-time attendance records. Remarkably, as the 1948 season drew to a close, no other franchise had followed their lead. In the minor leagues, Roy Campanella became the first black in the American Association, stopping at St. Paul before permanently joining Robinson on the Dodgers. Newcombe and Bankhead each won more than twenty games for Brooklyn affiliates. The Dodgers also added fleet-footed Sam Jethroe to the Montreal roster, where he batted .322. The Indians also began to stockpile black talent, signing future major leaguers Al Smith, Dave Hoskins, and Orestes

"Minnie" Minoso to minor league contracts. Several other blacks, including San Diego catcher John Ritchey, who broke the Pacific Coast League color line, played for independent teams.

In the interregnum between the 1948 and 1949 seasons four more teams—the Giants, Yankees, Braves, and Cubs—signed blacks to play in their farm systems, and 1949 would herald the beginning of widespread integration in the minor leagues. Blacks starred in all three Triple A leagues. In the Pacific Coast League, Luke Easter won acclaim as the "greatest natural hitter . . . since Ted Williams," amassing twenty-five home runs and ninety-two runs-batted-in in just eighty games before succumbing to a knee injury. Oakland's Artie Wilson led the league in hits, stolen bases, and batting average. In the International League, Jethroe scored 151 runs and stole eighty-nine bases, and Montreal teammate Dan Bankhead won twenty games for the second straight year. At Jersey City, Monte Irvin batted .373. The outstanding performer in the American Association was Ray Dandridge. Considered by many the greatest third baseman of all time, the acrobatic Dandridge, now in his late thirties, thrilled Minneapolis fans with his spectacular fielding, batting .364 in the process. Former Negro Leaguers turned in equally stellar performances at lower minor league levels as well.

By the end of the 1949 season, integration had achieved spectacular success at both the major and minor league level, but most teams moved "with all deliberate speed" in signing black players. The New York Giants joined the interracial ranks in 1949 when they promoted Monte Irvin and Hank Thompson. The following year, the Boston Braves purchased Jethroe from the Dodgers for one hundred thousand dollars and installed him in the starting lineup. In 1951 the Chicago White Sox acquired Minnie Minoso in a trade with Cleveland, and Bill Veeck, who had acquired the hapless St. Louis Browns, brought back Satchel Paige for another major league stint. Yet as late as August 1953, out of sixteen major league teams only these six fielded black players. Several teams displayed an interest in signing blacks but bypassed established Negro League stars who might have jumped directly to the majors, concentrating instead on younger prospects for the minor leagues. Still others like the Red Sox, Phillies, Cardinals, and Tigers continued to pursue a whites-only policy.

This failure to hire and promote blacks occurred amidst a continuing backdrop of outstanding performances by black players. The first generation of players from the Negro Leagues proved an extraordinary group. Jackie Robinson quickly established himself as one of the dominant stars in the national pastime. Sportswriters called him "the most dangerous man in baseball today." Campanella won accolades as the best catcher in the

National League and won the Most Valuable Player Award in 1951, 1953, and 1955. Pitcher Don Newcombe averaged better than twenty wins a season during his first five full years with the Dodgers. In addition, from 1950 to 1953 Negro League graduates Sam Jethroe, Willie Mays, Joe Black, and Jim Gilliam each won the National League Rookie of the Year Award.

In the American League, where integration proceeded at a slower pace, several players compiled outstanding records. Larry Doby, while never achieving the superstar status many expected, nonetheless became a steady producer, twice leading the league in home runs and five times driving in more than a hundred runs. His Cleveland teammate Luke Easter, who reached the majors in his mid-thirties, slugged eighty-six home runs and drove in three hundred runs in his brief three-season career. Satchel Paige, after a two-year stint with the Indians, joined the hapless St. Louis Browns from 1951 to 1953 and became one of the American League's best relief pitchers. On the Chicago White Sox, Minnie Minoso proved himself a consistent .300 hitter. Despite their relatively small numbers, teams with black players in both major leagues regularly finished high in the standings, and only in 1950 did both pennant winners field all-white squads. In addition, the more aggressive stance of National League teams in recruiting black players gave that circuit a clear superiority in World Series and All-Star contests for more than two decades.

By the end of the 1953 season, the benefits of integration had grown apparent to all but the most recalcitrant of major league owners. In September, the Chicago Cubs purchased shortstop Ernie Banks from the Kansas City Monarchs and finally elevated longtime minor league standout Gene Baker. Connie Mack's Philadelphia Athletics ended their Jim Crow era by acquiring pitcher Bob Trice. At the start of the 1954 season, the Washington Senators, St. Louis Cardinals, Pittsburgh Pirates, and Cincinnati Reds all joined the interracial ranks. The sudden integration of six more clubs left only the Yankees, Tigers, Phillies, and Red Sox with all-white personnel. In addition, 1954 marked the debut of young Henry Aaron with the Braves and the return of Willie Mays, who had sparkled for the Giants in 1951, from military service.

The desegregation of organized baseball opened the way not only to blacks in the United States but to those in other parts of the Americas as well. Throughout the twentieth century, baseball had imposed a curious double standard on Latin players, accepting those with light complexions but rejecting their darker countrymen. With the color barrier down, major league clubs found a wealth of talent in the Caribbean. Minnie Minoso, the "Cuban Comet" who integrated the Chicago White Sox, became the first

of the great Latin stars. Over a fifteen-year career, Minoso compiled a .298
batting average. In 1954 slick-fielding Puerto Rican Vic Power launched
his career with the Athletics. The following year, Roberto Clemente, the
greatest of the Latin stars, debuted with the Pittsburgh Pirates. The proud
Puerto Rican won four batting championships and amassed three thousand
hits en route to a .317 lifetime batting average. In the late 1950s the San
Francisco Giants revealed the previously ignored treasure trove that existed
in the Dominican Republic. In 1958 Felipe Alou became the first of three
Alou brothers to play for the Giants, and in 1960 the Giants unveiled pitcher
Juan Marichal, "the Dominican Dandy," who won 243 games en route to
the Hall of Fame.

Among the early Latin players were two sons of stars of the Jim Crow age.
Perucho Cepeda, who had won renown as "The Bull" in his native Puerto
Rico, had refused to play in the segregated Negro leagues. His son Orlando,
dubbed "The Baby Bull," went on to star for the Giants and Cardinals.
Luis Tiant, Sr., a standout performer in both Cuba and the Negro Leagues,
lived to see Luis Jr., win over two hundred major league games and excel
in the 1975 World Series.

As the major leagues moved slowly toward complete desegregation,
throughout the nation blacks invaded the minor leagues. In the northern
and western states, these athletes, a combination of youthful prospects and
Negro League veterans, were greeted by a storm of insults, beanballs, and
discrimination. "I learned more names than I thought we had," states Piper
Davis of his treatment by fans in the Pacific Coast League. At least a half-
dozen blacks had to be carried off the field on stretchers after being hit by
pitches between 1949 and 1951. In city after city, blacks found hotels and
restaurants unwilling to serve them.

"At the same time when they signed blacks and Latins," argues John
Roseboro about his Dodger employers, "they should have made sure they
would be welcome." But neither the Dodgers nor other clubs provided any
special assistance for their black farmhands. Despite these conditions blacks
compiled remarkable records in league after league. In the early 1950s blacks
overcame adversity and dominated the lists of batting leaders at the Triple
A level and in many of the lower circuits as well.

In 1952 blacks began to appear on minor league clubs in the Jim
Crow South. The Dallas Eagles of the Texas League, hoping to boost
sagging attendance, signed former Homestead Gray pitcher Dave Hoskins
to become the "Jackie Robinson of the Texas League." Hoskins took the
Lone Star State by storm, attracting record crowds en route to a 22-10 record.
The black pitcher posted a 2.12 earned run average and also finished third

in the league in batting with a .328 mark. By 1955 every Texas League club except Shreveport fielded black players.

Hoskins's performance inspired other teams throughout the South to scramble for black players. In 1953 nineteen-year-old Henry Aaron desegregated the South Atlantic League, which included clubs in Florida, Atlanta, and Georgia, and Bill White appeared in the Carolina League. Playing for Jacksonville (a city that seven years earlier had barred Jackie Robinson), Aaron "led the league in everything but hotel accommodations." By 1954, when the United States Supreme Court issued its historic *Brown* v. *Board of Education* decision ordering school desegregation, blacks had appeared in most Southern minor leagues.

The integration of the South, however, did not proceed without incidents. Black players recall these years as "an ordeal" or a "sentence" and described the South as "enemy country" or a "hellhole." In 1953 the Cotton States League barred brothers Jim and Leander Tugerson from competing. The following year, Nat Peeples broke the color line in the Southern Association but lasted only two weeks. For the remainder of the decade, the league adhered to a whites-only policy, a strategy that contributed to the collapse of the Southern Association in 1961. As resistance to the civil rights movement mounted in the 1950s, black players found themselves in increasingly hostile territory. Even in the pioneering Texas League, teams visiting Shreveport, Louisiana, in 1956 had to leave their black players at home due to stricter segregation laws.

In the face of these obstacles, young black stars like Aaron, Curt Flood, Frank Robinson, Bill White, and Leon Wagner overcame their frustrations "by taking it out on the ball." "What had started as a chance to test my baseball ability in a professional setting," wrote Curt Flood, "had become an obligation to test myself as a man." Throughout the 1950s blacks appeared regularly among the league leaders of the Texas, South Atlantic, Carolina, and other circuits, advancing both their own careers and the cause of integration.

As these events unfolded in the South, the major leagues completed their long overdue integration process. In 1955 the Yankees, after denying charges of racism for almost a decade, finally promoted Elston Howard to the parent club. Two more years passed before the Phillies integrated, and not until 1958 did a black player don a Tiger uniform. Thus, at the start of the 1959 season, only the Boston Red Sox, who had yet to hire either black scouts or representatives in the Caribbean, retained their Jim Crow heritage. A storm of protest arose when the Red Sox cut black infielder Elijah "Pumpsie" Green just before Opening Day, but on July 21, 1959, twelve years and 107 days after Jackie Robinson's Dodger debut, Green won promotion to the Boston club, completing the cycle of major league integration.

While integration became a reality in organized baseball, the Negro Leagues gradually faded into oblivion. As early as 1947 Negro League attendance, especially in cities close to National League parks, dropped precipitously. Negro League owners hoped to offset declining attendance by selling players to organized baseball, but major league teams paid what Effa Manley called "bargain basement" prices for all-star talent. In 1948 the Manleys' Newark Eagles and New York Black Yankees disbanded. The Homestead Grays severed all league connections and returned to its roots as a barnstorming unit. Without these teams, the Negro National League collapsed. A reorganized ten-team Negro American League, most of whose franchises were located in minor league cities, vowed to go on, but the spread of integration quickly thinned its ranks. By 1951 the league had dwindled to six teams. Two years later only the Birmingham Black Barons, Memphis Red Sox, Kansas City Monarchs, and Indianapolis Clowns remained.

For several years in the early 1950s, the Negro Leagues remained a breeding ground for young black talent. The New York Giants plucked Willie Mays from the roster of the Birmingham Black Barons, and the Boston Braves discovered Hank Aaron on the Indianapolis Clowns. The Kansas City Monarchs produced more than two dozen major leaguers, including Robinson, Paige, Banks, and Howard. But for most black players the demise of the Negro Leagues had disastrous effects. "The livelihoods, the careers, the families of 400 Negro ballplayers are in jeopardy," complained Effa Manley in 1948, "because four players were successful in getting into the major leagues." The slow pace of integration left most in a state of limbo, set adrift by their former teams but still unwelcomed in organized baseball. Some players like Buck Leonard and Cool Papa Bell were too old to be considered; others like Ray Dandridge and Piper Davis found themselves relegated to the minor leagues, where even outstanding records failed to win them promotion.

Throughout the 1950s the Negro American League struggled to survive, recruiting teenagers and second-rate talent for the modest four-team loop. In 1963 Kansas City hosted the thirtieth and last East-West All-Star Game, and the following year the famed Monarchs ceased touring the nation. By 1965 the Indianapolis Clowns remained as a last vestige of Jim Crow baseball. Utilizing white as well as black players, the Clowns continued for another decade. "We are all show now," explained their owner. "We clown, clown, clown."

But the legacy of the Negro Leagues remained. Robinson and other early black players introduced new elements of speed and "tricky baseball" into the major leagues, transforming and improving the quality of play. Since 1947, blacks have led the National League in stolen bases in all but two seasons. In the American League, a black or Latin baserunner has topped the league every year since 1951 with only two exceptions. Nor did this injection of speed come at the expense of power. In the 1950s and 1960s Hank Aaron, Willie Mays, and Frank Robinson reigned as the greatest power hitters in baseball. Thus, by the 1960s the national pastime more closely resembled the well-balanced offensive structure of the Negro Leagues than the unidimensional power-oriented attack that had typified the all-white majors.

The demise of the Negro Leagues and the decline of segregation in the majors, however, did not end discrimination. Conditions on and off the field, in spring training and in the executive suites, repeatedly reminded the black athletes of their second-class status. In the early 1950s all-white teams taunted their black opponents with racial insults. Blacks like Jackie and Frank Robinson, Minnie Minoso, and Luke Easter repeatedly appeared among the league leaders in being hit by pitches. While black superstars like Willie Mays had little difficulty ascending to the major leagues, players of only slightly above average talent found themselves buried for years in the minors. Many observers charged that teams had imposed quotas on the number of blacks they would field at one time.

In cities like St. Louis, Washington DC, and, later, Baltimore, black ballplayers could not stay at hotels with their teammates. In 1954 they achieved a breakthrough of sorts when the luxury Chase Hotel in St. Louis informed Jackie Robinson and other Dodger players that they could room there but had to refrain from using the dining room or swimming pool or loitering in the lobby. Ten years later the hotel had removed these restrictions but still relegated black players, according to Hank Aaron, to rooms "looking out over some old building or some green pastures or a blank wall, so nobody can see us through a window."

Blacks faced even greater discrimination each year in spring training in Florida. While all spring training sites now accepted blacks, segregation statutes and local traditions forced them to live in all-black boarding houses far from the luxury air-conditioned hotels that accommodated white players. "The whole set-up is wrong," protested Jackie Robinson. "There is no reason why we shouldn't be able to live with our teammates." When teams traveled from place to place, blacks could not join their fellow players in restaurants. Instead they had to wait on the bus until someone brought their food out to them. Some teams attempted to reduce the problems faced by blacks. Several clubs moved to Arizona, where conditions were only moderately improved. The Dodgers built a special spring training camp at Vero Beach, where players could live together. Most organizations, however, did very little to assist their black employees.

By the time that Jackie Robinson retired in 1956, conditions had barely improved. "After 10 years of traveling in the South," he charged, "I don't think advances have been fast enough. It's my belief that baseball itself hasn't done all it can to remedy the problems faced by . . . players." Over the next decade, a new generation of black players militantly demanded change. Cardinal stars Bill White, Curt Flood, and Bob Gibson protested against conditions in St. Petersburg, and Aaron and other black Braves demanded changes in Bradenton. In many instances, however, significant changes awaited passage of the Civil Rights Act of 1965 barring segregation in public facilities.

By 1960 Robinson, Campanella, Doby, and the cadre of Negro League veterans who had formed the vanguard of baseball integration had retired. In their wake a second generation of black players, most of whom had never appeared in the Negro Leagues, made most Americans forget that Jim Crow baseball had ever existed, as they shattered longstanding "unbreakable" records. In 1962 black shortstop Maury Wills stole 104 bases, eclipsing Ty Cobb's forty-seven-year-old stolen base mark. Twelve years later outfielder Lou Brock stole 118 bases en route to breaking Cobb's career stolen-base record as well. In 1966 Frank Robinson, who had won the National League Most Valuable Player Award in 1961, became the first player to win that honor in both leagues when he led the Baltimore Orioles to the American League pennant. By the end of his career, Robinson had slugged 586 home runs; only Babe Ruth among players of the Jim Crow era had hit more. Both Ernie Banks and Willie McCovey also amassed more than five hundred home runs during this era. On the pitcher's mound, the indomitable Bob Gibson proved himself one of the greatest strikeout pitchers in the game's history. Upon retirement, Gibson had amassed more strikeouts than anyone except Walter Johnson. Brock, Frank Robinson, Banks, McCovey, and Gibson all won election to the Hall of Fame in their first year of eligibility.

The greatness of these players notwithstanding, two other black players, Willie Mays and Hank Aaron, both of whom ironically had begun their careers in the Negro Leagues, reigned as the dominant stars of baseball in the 1950s and 1960s. Originally signed by the Birmingham Black Barons of the Negro American League, Mays had joined the New York Giants in midseason 1951, sparking their triumph in the most famous pennant race in history and winning the Rookie of the Year Award. After two years in the military he returned in 1954 to bat a league-leading .345 and hit forty-one home runs. The following year, he pounded fifty-one homers. A spectacular center fielder, Mays won widespread acclaim as the greatest all-around player in the history of the game. In 1969 he became only the second player in major league history to hit six hundred home runs and took aim at Babe Ruth's legendary lifetime total of 714. Over the next four seasons, the aging Mays added sixty more homers before retiring short of Ruth's record.

Unlike Mays, who had begun his career amidst the glare of the New York media, Hank Aaron had spent his career first in Milwaukee and later in Atlanta, far distant from the center of national publicity. Nonetheless, he steadily compiled record-threatening statistics in almost every offensive category. In 1972, at age thirty-eight, he surpassed Mays's home run total and set his sights on Ruth's. Entering the 1973 season, he needed just forty one home runs to catch the Babe. Performing under tremendous pressure and fanfare, Aaron stroked forty homers, leaving him just one shy of the record. He tied Ruth's mark with his first swing of the 1974 season. Three days later, on April 8, 1974, a nationwide television audience watched Aaron stroke home run number 715. Babe Ruth's "unreachable" record thus fell to a man whose career had started with the Indianapolis Clowns of the Negro Leagues. When Aaron retired in 1976 he boasted 755 home runs and held major league records for games played, at-bats, runs batted in, and extra-base hits. He also ranked second to Ty Cobb in hits and runs scored.

By the 1970s black players had become an accepted part of the baseball scene and regularly ranked among the most well-known symbols of the sport. Reggie Jackson, Willie Stargell, and Joe Morgan had succeeded Aaron, Mays, and the Robinsons as Hall of Fame–caliber superstars. Yet three decades after Jackie Robinson had broken the color barrier, racism and discrimination remained a persistent problem for baseball. Several studies demonstrated that baseball management channeled blacks into positions thought to require less thinking and fewer leadership qualities. In 1968 blacks accounted for more than half of the major league outfielders but only 20 percent of other position players. Black catchers were rare, and fewer than one in ten pitchers were black. By 1986 the disparity had grown greater. American-born blacks comprised 70 percent of all outfield positions but only 7 percent of all pitcher, second basemen, and third basemen positions. There were no American-born black catchers in the major leagues at the start of the 1986 season; the nineties, however, saw some progress with the appearance of Charles Johnson and Lenny Webster.

While superior black players had open access to the major leagues, those of average or slightly above average skills often found their paths blocked. "The Negro player may have to be better qualified than a white player to win the same position," argued Aaron Rosenblatt in 1967. "The undistinguished Negro player is less likely to play in the major leagues than the equally undistinguished white player." Rosenblatt demonstrated that black major leaguers on the whole batted twenty points higher than whites. As batting averages dropped, so did the proportion of blacks. This trend continued into the 1980s. A 1982 study revealed that 70 percent of all black nonpitchers were everyday starters, indicating a substantial bias against blacks who filled utility or pinch-hitting roles. Statistics compiled in 1986 showed a strikingly similar pattern.

The subtle nature of this on-the-field discrimination obscured it from public controversy. The failure of baseball to provide jobs for blacks in managerial and front-office positions, however, became an increasing embarrassment. In the early years of integration, baseball executives bypassed the substantial pool of experienced Negro Leaguers from consideration for managerial and coaching positions. A handful of blacks, including Sam Bankhead, Nate Moreland, Marvin Williams, and Chet Brewer managed independent, predominantly all-black teams in the minor leagues. The first generation of black major leaguers fared no better. "We bring dollars into club treasuries when we play," exclaimed Larry Doby, "but when we stop playing, our dollars stop." No major league organization hired a black pilot at any level until 1961 when the Pittsburgh Pirates placed Gene Baker at the helm of their Batavia franchise. By the mid-1960s no blacks had managed in the majors and only two had held full-time major league coaching positions. The first black umpire did not appear in the majors until 1966, when Emmett Ashford appeared in the American League.

In 1975 the Cleveland Indians hired Frank Robinson to be the first black major league manager. This precedent, however, opened few new doors. Robinson lasted two-and-a-half seasons with the Indians, later managed the San Francisco Giants for four years, and in 1988 was made manager of the Baltimore Orioles. Maury Wills and Larry Doby each had brief half-season stints as managers. After four decades of integration, only these three men had received major league managerial opportunities.

A similar situation existed in major league front offices. Only one black man, Bill Lucas of the Atlanta Braves, had served as a general manager. As late as 1982 a survey of twenty-four clubs (the Yankees and Red Sox refused to provide information) found that of 913 available white-collar baseball jobs, blacks held just 32 positions. Among 568 full-time major league scouts, only 15 were black. While many teams hired former players as announcers, few employed blacks in these roles. Five years later, conditions had not improved.

These shortcomings came to haunt baseball in 1987. Commissioner Peter Ueberroth had dedicated the season to the commemoration of the fortieth anniversary of Jackie Robinson's major league debut. As the celebration began, Los Angeles Dodger general manager Al Campanis questioned the ability of African Americans to assume managerial roles. When asked about the dearth of black managers, Campanis explained that blacks "may not have some of the necessities to be, let's say, a field manager or general manager." Campanis's statement, which surely reflected the thinking of many baseball executives, evoked a storm of protest and precipitated his resignation. An embarrassed Ueberroth pledged to take action to bring more blacks into leadership positions and hired University of California sociologist Harry Edwards to facilitate the process. Fifty blacks and Latins with past or present connections to baseball created their own Minority Baseball Network to apprise blacks of employment opportunities and to lobby clubs to recruit more minorities for front-office jobs.

When the controversy of 1987 had subsided, few franchises had taken significant steps to increase minority hiring. Several clubs added blacks to administrative positions, but none offered field or general manager positions to nonwhite candidates. In 1988 Frank Robinson received his third chance to manage in the major leagues, this time with the Baltimore Orioles. At midseason 1989 Cito Gaston assumed the reins of the Toronto Blue Jays. When the squads managed by Robinson and Gaston had their initial confrontation, it marked, after forty years of integration, the first time that two teams managed by black men had competed in a major league game. Fittingly, on the final weekend of the season, the Orioles and Blue Jays met face-to-face in a series to decide the championship of the American League Eastern Division. The spectacle offered a resounding rebuke to the shortsightedness and discrimination that continues to plague the national pastime.

By the 1993 season baseball seemed to have finally made some real progress in including minorities in its managerial ranks. The season saw five black and Hispanic field managers: Gaston, who after five years at the helm of the Blue Jays ranked as one of the most successful managers in baseball history, winning four divisional championships, two pennants, and two world championships; Felipe Alou, who led the Montreal Expos to consecutive second place finishes; Dusty Baker, who became the winningest rookie manager ever when his San Francisco Giants won 103 games (after winning only 72 games the year before); Don Baylor, who would pilot the expansion Colorado Rockies into the playoffs in only their third year of existence in 1995; and Tony Perez, who started the season as the manager of the Cincinnati Reds.

Progress extended into other areas of hiring as well. In 1994 Leonard Coleman succeeded Bill White as National League vice-president. By 1995, 27 percent of all coaches were black or latino. Minority hiring in the front office expanded to 17 percent in 1992, a level that held steady through 1994. The Houston Astros named Bob Watson their general manager, making him only the second black man to assume these responsibilities. Watson assumed the same position with the New York Yankees in 1996, and under his stewardship the club won the World Championship.

These undeniable gains, however, occurred against a backdrop of continuing racial controversy. The proportion of American-born black players in baseball's major leagues dropped from one in four in the late 1960s to only one in six in the late 1980s and 1990s. In minor league and college baseball, important sources of major league talent, the percentage of African Americans was even lower. Surveys indicated that African Americans, who had flocked to major league ballparks in the 1950s, now accounted for one out of every fourteen fans. Allegations that Cincinnati Reds owner Marge Schott had repeatedly used racial slurs (and that other owners had ignored these offenses) led to her suspension in 1993.

There remained no American minority owners of major league clubs. All twenty-eight chief executive officers were white. When Watson resigned after the 1997 season, there once again were no black general managers. The surge in the hiring of minority managers that had occurred in the early 1990s also seemed to have abated. Few African-American or Hispanic managers were hired after 1994.

During the early 1990s baseball undertook several initiatives to improve its image among minorities. The major leagues embraced John Young's RBI (Reviving Baseball in the Inner Cities) program, an effort to entice black youth away from other sports and back to the diamond. Attempts were also made to secure health benefits for surviving Negro League players. To achieve greater recognition for players from the Jim Crow era, the Hall of Fame instructed its Veterans Committee to honor one Negro League star a year for five years. As a result, Leon Day, Willie Wells, Bullet Joe Rogan and Turkey Stearnes were selected to enter the Hall. African-American reporter Wendell Smith was named to the writer's wing of the Hall of Fame. Nonetheless, when the five-year grace period ended, black athletes still remained woefully underrepresented at Cooperstown.

In 1997 baseball celebrated the fiftieth anniversary of what most consider its finest moment—Jackie Robinson's Brooklyn Dodger debut—with extraordinary and unprecedented fanfare. Major league baseball dedicated the season to Robinson's memory. Players wore arm patches honoring his achievements. Acting Baseball Commissioner Bud Selig announced that all teams would henceforth retire his number. On April 15, President Bill Clinton appeared between innings of a Los Angeles Dodger–New York Mets game at Shea Stadium to address the nation about Robinson's legacy.

A year later the National Baseball Hall of Fame added Larry Doby, who broke the American League color line, and Baltimore Afro-American sportswriter Sam Lacy to its rolls. At times the commemorations threatened to be overwhelmed by nostalgia and commercialism. Overall, however, the 1997 festivities reminded the nation once again of its past heritage—both the shameful and the heroic—and its ongoing obligations to seek greater equality in the future.

At the turn of the century, however, baseball continued to make incremental progress, at best, in alleviating the remnants of discrimination in managerial hiring. The paradoxical aftermath of the 2000 season amply illustrates the lingering problem. Only five of the thirty major league teams employed nonwhite managers in 2000. Two of them, Dusty Baker of the San Francisco Giants and Jerry Manuel of the Chicago White Sox, unexpectedly led their teams to division championships and the best records in their respective leagues. Baker and Manuel both won Manager of the Year Awards—Baker for the third time in nine years.

Yet only one of the six teams with managerial vacancies—the Pittsburgh Pirates who hired Lloyd McClendon—offered a position to a minority candidate. When the White Sox named Kenny Williams as general manager, he became the first African American to hold that job in the major leagues since Bob Watson left the Yankees prior to the 1998 season, and only the third in major league history. Although parity seemed more evident on the playing field, the front office remained only a frontier, rather than a stronghold, of equality.

3
REFLECTIONS ON BASEBALL HISTORY

NINE

Playing by the Book

Baseball History in the 1980s

In 1983, when excerpts from my book *Baseball's Great Experiment* appeared in *Sports Illustrated*, I found myself the subject of the weekly "Letter from the Publisher." I posed for a baseball fan's rendezvous with destiny with a stickball bat resting comfortably on my shoulder and a shirt emblazoned with the symbol of my Pacific Ghost League team. I prepared pithy quotes. "Being a baseball fan is great training for a historian," I sagely observed. "The types of things I did as a kid—learning the statistics of the players and the folklore of the game—have served me well."[1] I meant this statement as a throwaway line, to be taken half-seriously. In retrospect, however, I have grown convinced of its validity. To be a baseball fan, by the very nature of the game, with its emphasis on records, summers past, and bygone heroes, is to be a historian.

An abundant baseball literature affirms this assertion. Since the days of Henry Chadwick, journalists and fans have authored comprehensive chronicles and popular biographies. The Society for American Baseball Research (SABR) has unleashed thousands of researchers to "recreate" baseball history. Yet only recently have trained academic historians applied the skills of our craft to an analysis of the national pastime. In doing so, we have hopefully created a genre that supplements, rather than duplicates, nonacademic efforts by applying the standards of the professional historian to the study of baseball.

What are these standards? Harold Seymour, who in 1960 wrote the first scholarly treatment of the national pastime, offered an excellent set of guidelines in his introduction. Baseball, he charged, "has been badly served by history," in books "put together after only the most cursory kind of research." He based his own work, on the other hand, "on wide research into the sources of baseball history which were examined—many of them for the first time—in libraries and archives in various parts of the country." His history of baseball, Seymour asserted, "describes the growth of the game from the perspective of American history." Baseball thus became a "microcosm of America," a reflection of the national transition to urbanism, professionalism, and commercialism, which accompanied industrial capitalism. Seymour includes the players, teams, and pennant races, but he "subordinates these to the economic and social aspects of baseball and its development as a part of Americana."[2]

Thus Seymour laid out three critical distinctions between popular and scholarly history. First, academically trained historians apply a more stringent research methodology, relying not simply on the oral folklore of the game, but on exhaustive archival and newspaper research. The historian must seek, wherever possible, new, previously untapped sources that yield new information and/or fresh insights into timeworn tales. Second, any analysis of the evolution of baseball must be placed in the context of American history. Changes in the national pastime often accompanied broader national developments. This includes not only the obvious parallels of race relations and business practices, but changing styles of play, player personalities, and cultural messages. Each new rule may not have possessed profound social significance, but as Allen Guttmann has demonstrated, the very willingness to alter fundamental strictures reflected the emerging rationality of modern society as opposed to the ritualistic nature of traditional sports.[3] Third, and perhaps most important, scholarly research deals not simply in facts and chronology, but in analysis and interpretation. The academic, building on the work of earlier scholars, identifies historically significant themes and issues, the study of which will enhance our understanding of both baseball and America.

In writing baseball history academics have not monopolized these criteria. Books like Eliot Asinof's *Eight Men Out*, a fine study of the 1919 Black Sox Scandal, Robert Peterson's *Only the Ball Was White*, a pathbreaking history of the Negro Leagues, and Roger Kahn's *The Boys of Summer*, a retrospective account of major league baseball's first racially integrated team, stand as excellent historical studies.[4] Sections of the wonderfully idiosyncratic Bill James Historical Baseball Abstract, with its use of old baseball guides, sharp analytical intelligence, and dogged dedication to answering questions large and small, also survive these more stringent standards.[5] But far too many of the books that pass as baseball history and biography uncritically accept the unsubstantiated recollections of eyewitnesses or report only the hits, runs, and especially the errors of earlier accounts.

Seymour made two additional comments worth noting about baseball history. His work, he wrote, "is the product of a lifetime love of baseball that began as a boyhood enthusiasm and developed into the mature interest of the professional historian."[6] This description typifies virtually all who followed him into this arena. As fans and devotees of the game, writing baseball allows us, in a limited fashion, to become a part of the game not as it is played, but as it enters into the mainstream of American culture. As a result, the study of baseball offers a striking opportunity. Seymour attempted, not entirely successfully, to create a book addressed not to "specialists," but aimed at a broader audience of baseball enthusiasts.[7] This, then, should be the final goal of the academic baseball historian: to create a readily accessible and readable literature that not only adheres to the standards of our profession, but that introduces the craft and relevance of history to those not normally exposed to the discipline.

In the 1980s university trained historians, primarily those publishing in academic presses, have followed in the footsteps of Seymour to create a distinct body of baseball literature. Like Seymour and David Voigt, who has also authored a multivolume history of the national pastime,[8] these writers have focused largely on the professional major leagues, both black and white, rather than on baseball as it was played in the towns and on the campuses, schoolyards, and sandlots of America.[9] An assessment of these scholarly works must, by definition, judge them for their contributions to the study of both history and baseball.[10]

In many ways, *Touching Base: Professional Baseball and American Culture in the Progressive Era* by Steven Riess represents the most ambitious of these efforts.[11] Riess wrote not from the perspective of a sports historian, but as a disciple of the "new urban history." Firmly grounded in the historiography of the 1960s and 1970s, Riess addressed issues of immigration, social control, social mobility, and political machinery as manifested in the rise of baseball in New York, Chicago, and Atlanta. Using methodologies pioneered by Stephan Thernstrom[12] and other students of occupational and residential mobility, Riess became the first historian to apply quantitative techniques in his analysis of those who played the game.

Riess contrasted the democratic and egalitarian rhetoric of baseball's boosters with the realities of the emerging professional sport. Baseball in the early twentieth century remained an entertainment for the native-born middle class. Few of the "new immigrants" from Eastern Europe attended baseball contests and rarely did members of these groups appear in the major leagues. Nor did baseball provide a significant source of social mobility. Most ballplayers came from middle class and lower middle class backgrounds and were far better educated than the typical American worker.

Owners of professional baseball franchises, who stressed the honesty and wholesomeness of their sport, relied heavily on connections with Democratic political machines in cities like New York and Chicago and often found themselves drawn into the corrupt alliance of gamblers, political bosses, and real estate and streetcar speculators, who dictated urban growth during this era. Nonetheless, argues Riess, despite the "substantial disparity that existed between the ideology of baseball . . . and the realities of the game . . . baseball operated as a means of describing and reinforcing the values that regulated behavior and goal achievement as well as determining suitable solutions to certain social problems."[13]

Touching Base, by addressing issues in the mainstream of historical thought and in its thorough and often innovative research techniques, marked an auspicious beginning for a "new" baseball history. Yet on another major level, it failed. Repetitious and poorly written, it held little attraction for those outside the academic community.

Like *Touching Base*, Richard Crepeau's *Baseball: America's Diamond Mind, 1919–1941* appeared in 1980.[14] Crepeau emulates writers like Henry Nash Smith and Leo Marx, seeking societal truths from cultural images.[15] He looked not at baseball itself, but at the "cultural values" that "people connected with game" attempted to project. "This book is not a history of baseball," wrote Crepeau. "It is an attempt to look at one segment of American society as it saw itself and as it reflected the larger society."[16] A study of baseball, the "undisputed National Pastime," might reveal what Americans perceived to be the "ethos" of their society.

Relying primarily on images surveyed in *The Sporting News*, Crepeau produced an enlightening and entertaining book, but one with few surprises. In the aftermath of the Black Sox Scandal, "baseball entered the Twenties preparing to defend standards, ethics, morals, patriotism and the remaining eternal verities." Organized baseball portrayed itself as a democratic game, a meritocracy that rewarded the work ethic and offered unlimited opportunities. In an age of rapid urbanization and change, "it remained unabashedly committed to the older 'American Way,'" clinging to the "rural values of the nineteenth century." As the nation struggled through the Great Depression, baseball became a "restorer of confidence," and as foreign affairs gained greater significance, baseball emerged as an "exporter of American values." Thus World War II was fought "to make the world safe for both baseball and democracy."[17]

Crepeau's most interesting and controversial arguments utilize baseball players as symbols of their times. Babe Ruth achieved this immense popularity, according to Crepeau, because he "refused to be reshaped and become one of the faceless urban mass or made over into a company man." Ruth represented "a screaming symbol . . . the last gasp of the rugged individual." In the 1930s, however, Joe DiMaggio personified the new order. A "colorless superstar" of "flawless perfection," DiMaggio was "the corporate player," baseball's version of the "man in the gray flannel suit."[18] Those who watched Ruth and DiMaggio perform may well question these judgments, but for Crepeau what is significant is not their athletic excellence, but the manner in which sportswriters and others portrayed them.

Perhaps the most common theme in the academic literature involves the emergence of baseball as a business. "Contrary to widespread belief," wrote Seymour in the opening lines of his two-volume history, "professional baseball is not a sport. It is a commercialized amusement business."[19] Seymour devoted a large part of his work to the entrepreneurial organization of baseball—the launching of the National League, the rise of the reserve clause, labor relations, administrative problems, the rise of the farm system, and other business related matters. In 1965 economic Ralph Andreano added a perceptive analysis of nineteenth-century baseball entrepreneurs. These men, wrote Andreano, established the "three most important elements of baseball's structure as a professional sport and business . . . territorial rights, the reserve rule, and internal self-regulation."[20] Both Riess and Crepeau also devoted considerable attention to the economic and financial aspects of the national pastime.

In 1980 historian Lee Lowenfish teamed with former major leaguer Tony Lupien to produce *The Imperfect Diamond: The Story of Baseball's Reserve System and the Men Who Fought to Change It.*[21] The first complete history of labor relations in the sport, with an admitted "perspective sympathetic to the player," Lowenfish and Lupien traced the fight against the reserve clause from the Brotherhood War of 1889–1890 to the 1976 Messermith-McNally decision creating free agency. *The Imperfect Diamond* included accounts of early union efforts, the "prophetic failure" of Robert Murphy's American Baseball Guild of 1946, challenges to the reserve clause by Danny Gardella and Curt Flood, and the development of the current Major League Baseball Players Association under the direction of Marvin Miller.

The Imperfect Diamond, aiming more at a popular than a scholarly audience, had much in common with traditional baseball chronicles. The events described seemingly possessed no relevance beyond baseball's domain. Lowenfish and Lupien make no effort to place baseball's "peculiar institution" into the context of labor history or American history in general. Nor do they define critical historical issues outside of the immediate reserve clause struggle. Yet in their choice of subject matter, diligent research, and attention to oft-ignored episodes of player-owner conflict, Lowenfish and Lupien have greatly enhanced our understanding of the history of labor relations in organized baseball.

Two biographies, *A. G. Spalding and the Rise of Baseball: The Promise of American Sport* by Peter Levine and *Ban Johnson: Czar of Baseball* by Eugene Murdock deal with the management side of the equation.[22] Since Spalding dominated the National League in the 1880s and 1890s and Johnson, the founder of the American League, succeeded him as the most powerful figure in the sport, these books offer a fascinating overview of the first half-century of major league baseball. While Levine makes far better use of the work of other historians, both books offer thorough research and provocative analysis.

Spalding, Levine argues convincingly, "was the key figure in the establishment of the white world of professional baseball as a viable commercial enterprise and as an acceptable pastime for Victorian America."[23] In this Levine echoes the earlier assessment of Andreano, who ranked Spalding's managerial and organizational acumen "on a par with the achievements of the Rockefellers, Mellons, Morgans, and the like."[24] For Levine, however, the true significance of Spalding rests "in the manner in which his personal story intersected with the larger culture." Spalding emerges as the quintessential product of industrializing America. Like an upwardly mobile skilled artisan of the age, Spalding, one of baseball's first great stars, rose through the ranks to become a manager, a team owner, and a dominant force in the founding and perpetuation of the National League. Spalding, states Levine, "came of age in a society fascinated with notions of career and with the importance of efficient organization and the leadership of trained experts." He applied these tenets to both baseball and the sporting goods industry with spectacular success. In addition, Spalding became one of the leading promoters of the ideology that sport, as an antidote to the evils of the city, a cure for the frenetic pace of American life, and a means of controlling immigrants and workers, "served a significant social purpose." To Spalding baseball and other sports were crucial in the development of "uniquely American values and character traits." Spalding's campaign to legitimize sport, as Levine notes, "was clearly self-serving: it nurtured his material interests and his considerable demand for public attention." But it also accurately reflected the beliefs of Spalding and a whole generation of moral reformers.[25]

Spalding thus emerges as a mirror of nineteenth-century social values and a historic industrial innovator. Levine pursues these themes through a primarily topical analysis of Spalding's career from his boyhood in Rockford,

Illinois, where he absorbed the town's typical nineteenth-century "booster mentality," his career as a player, his acquisition and management of the Chicago White Stockings, his role as "the brains of the National League," and the creation of A. G. Spalding and Brothers. The topical, rather than chronological, approach results in a major weakness of an otherwise well conceived and executed work. By dividing Spalding's multiple roles into separate chapters, rather than allowing them to emerge simultaneously as they did in real life, Levine unintentionally obscures critical linkages and generates unnecessary repetition, minimizing the appeal of his book to a non-academic audience.

Levine also makes no effort to reconcile Spalding's public image with the realities of his private affairs. Near the end of the book, the reader learns in passing that Spalding, the defender of American values and morality, had a long-term extramarital affair that produced an illegitimate son. A greater effort to explain contradictions in Spalding's personality, developed within the context of the broader tale of entrepreneurial exploits, would have made this a far more interesting work. Nonetheless, *A. G. Spalding and the Rise of Baseball* represents a fine example of the potentialities of baseball history.

Spalding's retirement as a baseball executive in 1902 coincided with the rise of Ban Johnson, the subject of Murdock's biography. Johnson, after successfully guiding the new American League into a profitable alliance with the older circuit in 1903, dominated major league baseball until the appointment of Kenesaw Mountain Landis in 1922. Unlike Levine, Murdock does not attempt to assess Johnson's significance beyond baseball, but confines his account to the "czar's" contributions to the game. Murdock provides the most detailed account available of "war" between the National and American Leagues and of Johnson's dealings with players, umpires, and rival leagues. He offers a sympathetic portrayal of Johnson's conflicts with Landis and his forced retirement in 1927, concluding that "he did not leave when his work was done," and thus "invited the final indignity." Indeed, Murdock frequently acts as Johnson's advocate rather than an impartial biographer, defending both his actions and his role as "the foremost of the founding fathers of baseball," a somewhat exaggerated assessment.[26]

Both Levine and Murdock chose baseball executives as the focus of their research, emphasizing how the baseball experience fit into the general pattern of American business history. Selecting a baseball player as the subject of a scholarly biography, on the other hand, poses a fundamental problem. With the rare exception of a Jackie Robinson, whose relevance clearly transcended athletics, are ballplayers really historically significant figures? In 1975 Marshall Smelser, best known as a historian of the early republic, defended his choice of Babe Ruth as the subject of a biography by invoking Ruth's very prominence in American folklore. "He is our Hercules, our Samson, Beowulf, Siegfried," argued Smelser. "No other person outside of public life so stirred our imaginations or so captured our affections." Can the same be said of other players?

Along with Ruth, Ty Cobb ranks as baseball's leading immortal, the greatest player of his age and perhaps of all time. Charles C. Alexander, in *Ty Cobb*, applied the historian's touch to "The Georgia Peach."[27] The result is a well-researched and engagingly written, but ultimately disappointing book. Alexander's season-by-season account dwells too much on batting achievements and pennant races. As a result Cobb never establishes himself as a significant figure beyond the realm of baseball. "A deeply flawed, fascinating personality," Cobb emerges as neither symbol nor signpost. Alexander's central theme seems to be that Cobb "was the most volatile, the most fear inspiring presence ever to appear on a baseball field."[28] Yet this, in and of itself, does not command historical attention.

Beyond business and biography, the other most frequently visited aspect of baseball history in the 1980s was the bittersweet saga of the Negro Leagues. Those of us who discovered baseball during our formative years in the 1950s confronted a paradox that our youthful minds could not quite appreciate. We knew of Jackie Robinson and his heroic efforts to end segregation, and we gloried in the achievements of black players, who only a decade earlier could never have appeared in a big league game. Yet we had no sense of where the Roy Campanellas and Don Newcombes, the Larry Dobys and Monte Irvins, had learned their craft and polished their skills while awaiting the call of the majors. For most of us, these players had materialized out of thin air, sent by the gods of baseball to thrill and delight and to usher in a golden age of brotherhood and base stealing. That there had once existed a flourishing domain in America known as the Negro Leagues had been instantly forgotten. That several teams still struggled on the margins of the national pastime would have greatly surprised us.

Thus, the Negro Leagues, "invisible" during their best years, almost totally disappeared from American memory in the 1950s and 1960s. Even in the black community, baseball fans savored the hard-won fruits of integration and turned their gaze away from the legacy of black baseball. "The big league doors suddenly opened one day," wrote sportswriter Wendell Smith, "and when Negro players walked in, Negro baseball walked out."[29] Not until 1970, when Robert Peterson published his pathbreaking *Only the Ball Was White*,[30] did the veil that had dropped over the Negro Leagues begin to lift. Today, while the stars of black baseball remain underrepresented in the Hall of Fame, they have received a far fairer share of attention in the literature of the past several decades, giving us a broad appreciation of the role of the Negro Leagues in baseball history and in the culture and community they served.

Nowhere is the neglect of the Negro Leagues more apparent than in the two primary academic histories of baseball. Both Harold Seymour and David Voigt in their multivolume studies deal briefly with the exclusion of blacks in the 1880s. Black ballplayers then disappear from both narratives, reappearing again only in volume 2 of Voigt's work in a brief prelude to the Robinson saga.[31] The Negro Leagues fared no better in accounts of baseball integration. Most biographies of Robinson written in the 1950s, including Robinson's own *Wait Till Next Year*, coauthored with Carl Rowan, mention his stint with the Kansas City Monarchs but provide few details other than a critique of the heavy travel schedule and loose style of play.[32]

Those determined to learn more about the Negro Leagues in the 1950s and 1960s had to search diligently. The standard work on the topic was *Sol White's Official Baseball Guide*. White, a former professional player, chronicled the nineteenth-century travails of blacks in organized baseball, their ultimate exclusion, and the formation of early black barnstorming clubs. But White's book, originally published in 1907, had long since passed out of print.[33]

Brief glimpses of life in the Negro Leagues could be found in at least two of the books about the first blacks to cross baseball's color line. Although "Doc" Young's 1953 volume, *Great Negro Baseball Stars and How They Made the Major Leagues*, focused primarily on those players who had advanced from the Negro Leagues into the majors, chapters on the black stars of the preintegration era and those in the minors offered insightful information. A skillful, perceptive writer, whose talents rank him with Wendell Smith and Sam Lacy, the deans of black sports writing, Young presents an introduction to the stars, if not the world of, black baseball.[34] In 1964 Jackie Robinson provided another overview of the integration process in *Baseball Has Done It*. This wonderfully revealing collection of interviews with black major leaguers also included reminiscences by Negro League stars Terris McDuffie and Bill Yancey.[35]

Player autobiographies offered other information on black baseball. Roy Campanella's *It's Good to Be Alive* (1959) gave one of the best accounts of life in the Negro Leagues. Campanella's tale, still fascinating reading, also introduces the reader to barnstorming in the United States and to winter ball in the Caribbean.[36] Far less enlightening is Satchel Paige's autobiographical effort, *Maybe I'll Pitch Forever*, published in 1962. Paige's legendary reputation had always transcended the Negro Leagues, and his brief but successful major league stint had firmly fixed him in the public mind. Writing in a folksy style, fully in keeping with the image he had long cultivated, Paige and coauthor David Lipman dwelled more on the pitcher's skills, eccentricities, and exploits than black baseball itself. Nonetheless, the weak administrative structure of the Negro Leagues and the team-hopping habits of the players are readily apparent.[37]

For the remainder of the sixties, books about the Negro Leagues or books even mentioning the era of black baseball remained rare. Both Willie Mays and Hank Aaron devoted a few pages to their brief tenures with the Birmingham Black Barons and Indianapolis Clowns respectively in their autobiographies, *Willie Mays: My Life In and Out of Baseball* (1966) and *Aaron, r.f.* (1968).[38] Jack Orr included a chapter on the Negro Leagues in *The Black Athlete* in 1969.[39] Little existed to sate the curiosity of those who remembered black baseball or of younger people who had seen references to it.

The long drought came to an end with the publication of Peterson's *Only the Ball Was White.* Poring over black newspapers and interviewing former players, Peterson painstakingly pieced together the history of blacks in baseball from the days of Bud Fowler, a nineteenth-century second baseman, to Jackie Robinson's historic breakthrough. Peterson introduced a new generation of readers to John Henry Lloyd, "Cool Papa" Bell, Rube Foster, and a host of other Negro League stars. Appendices to *Only the Ball Was White* included capsule biographies of Negro League greats, year-by-year standings for the leagues, box scores for the East-West All-Star Games, and an alphabetical listing of hundreds of players and the teams they had performed for.[40] Peterson's book, still the best overview of the subject, marked a watershed in the historiography of the Negro Leagues, opening up a broader interest in the research of others and spawning a new generation of Negro League historians, most of whom had never seen a segregated contest.

Two events in 1971 further contributed to the sudden growth of interest in black baseball. The National Baseball Hall of Fame, succumbing to pressures from fans and media, belatedly began to recognize the Negro Leagues by admitting Satchel Paige and setting up a Negro League committee to consider additional nominees. (The Hall of Fame insensitively planned to commemorate these stars in a separate section until protests of "Jim Crow" forced full inclusion.) In August 1971 the "Cooperstown 16" launched the Society for American Baseball Research (SABR). As the organization grew, it established a Negro League committee to coordinate research and facilitate communication among members interested in black baseball. SABR journals, most notably the annual *Baseball Research Journal* and later the *National Pastime*, offered a place for Negro League writers to publish their works and a forum for discussion.

The new breed of Negro League aficionados faced a difficult task in recreating baseball in the Jim Crow era. As Peterson had warned, unearthing the history of the Negro Leagues "was like trying to find a single black strand through a ton of spaghetti."[41] Team records were largely unavailable. Major newspapers and mainstream sports journals like the *Sporting News* had rarely covered black games. Black newspapers like the *Pittsburgh Courier* and *Chicago Defender* offered a more promising source, but only major public and university libraries held significant collections of back issues. As a result, oral history became the primary tool of the Negro League chroniclers.

The most prolific of the interviewers was John Holway, whose *Voices from the Great Black Baseball Leagues* (1975) became the model for the genre. Holway had sought out Negro Leaguers since the 1960s, and his collection includes talks with eighteen players and Effa Manley, the former owner of the Newark Eagles. Using their own words, the black athletes brought alive the itinerant lifestyle and flamboyant play of the Negro Leagues. One controversial theme ran through both the player accounts and Holway's writing: that in the age of Jim Crow the quality of black baseball was equal, if not superior, to the major league variety. In addition to editing the colorful accounts of the long-forgotten stars, Holway compiled records of games between black players and major league squads between 1886 and 1948. In the 445 contests that he unearthed, Holway discovered that blacks had won 269 and lost only 172, with 4 ties.[42]

In 1973 two unique and entertaining looks at the Negro Leagues appeared simultaneously. *Some Are Called Clowns* by Bill Heward is one of the most unusual and delightful baseball books ever written. Heward, an aspiring pitcher, described his three seasons in the early 1970s with the Indianapolis Clowns, the final remnant of the old Negro Leagues. Heward complements his own experiences on the barnstorming tour with a keen sense of the club's history. The result is a fine blend of entertainment and analysis, a glimpse into a dying world that has now passed into oblivion.[43] Novelist William Brashler offered another look at black barnstormers in *The Bingo Long Traveling All-Stars and Motor Kings*, a fictional account that became a very entertaining feature film.[44]

By the mid-1970s national interest in black baseball had reached a level surpassing anything that had existed while the leagues were still alive. Long ignored by the media and the baseball establishment, players like Buck

Leonard, Ray Dandridge, and Willie Wells found themselves besieged by amateur and sometimes professional historians armed with tape recorders. Interviews with former Negro League players began to appear in numerous regional and national periodicals and in SABR publications.[45]

Art Rust, Jr., combined his own reminiscences with those of Negro League players in *"Get That Nigger Off the Field"*.[46] Two books by Negro League participants supplemented the work of the oral historians. In 1976 Effa Manley published her own account, *Negro Baseball... Before Integration*, which unfortunately proved far less outspoken and interesting than the author herself.[47] Quincey Trouppe, a former catcher, who had once had a "cup of coffee" in the majors, offered his autobiography *20 Years Too Soon*, lovingly recreating his decades in the Negro Leagues, on the barnstorming tours, in Latin America, and finally in organized baseball. Trouppe's book, generously decorated with photographs from his scrapbooks, contains a wealth of information about black players and black baseball.

The oral histories and autobiographies of the 1970s and 1980s capture the flavor of life in the Negro Leagues and greatly enhance our knowledge, but as analytical tools they have severe limitations. Human memories tend toward the exaggerated and romantic. They deal largely with selected moments and places rather than the broader picture. As oral history piles upon oral history, the reader often receives variations on the same theme with little focus or historical direction. Contrary to popular opinion, oral histories do not speak for themselves; they require commentary to place them into historical perspective.

Often good biographies will provide this perspective, but book length chronicles of Negro League stars have been rare. In 1978 William Brashler published *Josh Gibson: A Life in the Negro Leagues*, a good effort that amply demonstrates the pitfalls of books of this type. Brashler knows the Negro Leagues and writes well but apparently could not gather enough information to fill a book about the great catcher. This slim volume includes both Brashler's personal recollections (not of Gibson, but of Ted Williams) and a chapter on what happened to Gibson's best friend, Sam Bankhead, after Gibson's death. Thus Brashler's book is pleasurable and, in spots, revealing, but ultimately unsatisfying.[48]

In the early 1980s academia belatedly discovered the Negro Leagues.[49] My own volume on baseball integration, *Baseball's Great Experiment: Jackie Robinson and His Legacy*, appeared in 1983. Although primarily concerned with black players in organized baseball, the Negro Leagues took their rightful place as an integral part of the story. In the 1940s and 1950s they became the fount of major and minor league talent, an important transitional agency in the recruitment of black players. I chronicled their ultimate decline and the fate of the great black stars of that age and analyzed the manner in which Negro League playing styles transformed the national pastime and improved the game.[50]

Baseball's Great Experiment was published simultaneously with Donn Rogosin's *Invisible Men: Life in Baseball's Negro Leagues,* the first major overview of the Negro Leagues since Peterson's book. Rogosin's lively narrative demonstrates the importance of baseball not only to African Americans, but also to the hundreds of towns and cities, both in the United States and the Caribbean, where barnstorming squads enlivened athletic competition. Rogosin deals with the origins of the ballplayers and what a baseball career meant in the black community. Rogosin's central themes involve the "irrationality" of segregation as seen through baseball and the role that the Negro Leagues played in the battle for integration. But it is his emphasis on social and cultural issues that makes *Invisible Men* a valuable supplement to, rather than a duplication of, Peterson's *Only the Ball Was White.*[51]

Much of the appeal of *Invisible Men* derives from Rogosin's skillful use of oral history, which captures the lively personalities of the Negro League veterans. Yet therein also lies the book's greatest weakness. At times Rogosin accepts these testimonies too readily and completely. In addition, Rogosin's work lacks documentation and a bibiliography, critical failings in a historical work, even one written for a popular audience.

While both Rogosin's book and my own received widespread publicity, another study, *The Kansas City Monarchs: Champions of Black Baseball* by Janet Bruce, went largely unnoticed. This is unfortunate because not only has Bruce produced one of the best books about the Negro Leagues, but her work, though flawed, marks an important new direction for baseball history in general. Organizationally, particularly in the early chapters, *The Kansas City Monarchs* could be greatly improved and Bruce tends too often toward the anachronistic quote—citing players who played in the 1940s to prove points about the 1920s and 1930s. But Bruce more than makes up for this with her extensive research. Utilizing archival collections, personal papers, black newspapers and numerous interviews, she also displays a keen awareness of prior historical works on baseball, Kansas City, and black America.[52]

For Bruce, "the Monarchs were a major social institution for black Kansas Citians," a symbol that people "from every walk of life" rallied around. As bartender Jesse Fisher states, "they were the life of Kansas City in the Negro vicinity." Bruce skillfully examines this relationship between team and community. Monarch home games, writes Bruce, "were great social gatherings." The players themselves ranked among the most respected blacks in the city, role models for Kansas City's youth. "For Black Kansas Citians crushed hard by discrimination," concludes Bruce, "The Monarchs became a community focus."[53] Bruce supplements this central theme with a fine discussion of the financial and administrative tasks of running a baseball team, a lively description of barnstorming, and an analysis of life in the Negro Leagues in the aftermath of integration. *The Kansas City Monarchs* offers both a model for future histories of individual clubs and a valuable social commentary.

Rob Ruck, in *Sandlot Seasons* takes a similar yet equally original approach. Ruck examines the black athletic experience in Pittsburgh, the capital of black baseball, emphasizing both professional sports and their relationship to the games played on the sandlots. Pittsburgh hosted both the legendary Pittsburgh Crawfords and Homestead Grays, and Ruck has combined perceptive team histories with a fascinating portrait of the role that sports played in Pittsburgh's black community. Populated by neighborhood athletic legends and Negro League superstars, ministers and numbers runners, bourgeoisie and unskilled laborers, *Sandlot Seasons* is a work of originality and insight.[54]

Bruce and Ruck, in their evocation of Kansas City and Pittsburgh, have produced not just baseball histories, but thoughtful community studies. Sportswriters, politicians, and sociologists have often claimed that a franchise offers profound psychic and financial benefits to towns and cities, but rarely has anyone attempted to test this assumption, particularly in a historical context. *The Kansas City Monarchs* and *Sandlot Seasons* illustrate the potential of baseball as an entrée into the dynamics of community life.

Thus, after several decades of baseball integration and twenty years of relative obscurity, the Negro Leagues have become a fertile ground for both baseball history and broader sociological approaches.[55] Black baseball has attracted both widespread interest among baseball "buffs" and a level of respectability in academia. But those who tread in this arena must also bear in mind the ultimate irony of baseball integration. The Jackie Robinson saga stands as one of the most sacrosanct in our folklore. It symbolizes American fair play and the beginning of the end for the national disgrace that was Jim Crow. The universal acceptance of blacks in baseball stands as a testament to the achievement of Robinson and those who followed him. No one would question that the disappearance of the Negro Leagues marked a step forward in our social evolution. Yet something vital and distinctively

American died with the passing of black baseball. At their height, the Negro Leagues were a two million dollar empire, largely controlled by blacks, employing hundreds of players and offering a form of cultural identification to millions of fans. Today more blacks play in the major leagues, yet fewer make their living from baseball. Black athletes serve as role models for both black and white youth, but they do so in an economic and organizational context far removed from their own ethnic and racial communities.

The first generation of serious scholarship amply demonstrates the promise and the pitfalls of baseball history. For the most part, these studies have satisfied the demands of the profession. They raise questions and generate monographs that address issues in the mainstream of historical thought and adhere to the established standards of research and evidence. On another level, however, the new baseball literature has been less successful. Few of these volumes hold significant appeal for the nonacademic reader. Baseball history presents a rare opportunity to expand the audience for scholarly work. Future authors should bear this in mind as they translate their "boyhood (and girlhood) enthusiasm . . . into the mature interest of the professional historian."

NOTES

1. "Letter from the Publisher," *Sports Illustrated* 58, June 20, 1983, 4.

2. Harold Seymour, *Baseball: The Early Years* (New York: Oxford University Press, 1960), v–vii. See also Seymour, *Baseball: The Golden Age* (New York: Oxford University Press, 1971).

3. Allen Guttmann, *From Ritual to Record: The Nature of Modern Sports* (New York: Columbia University Press, 1978).

4. Eliot Asinof, *Eight Men Out: The Black Sox and the 1919 World Series* (New York: Holt, Rinehart and Winston, 1963); Robert Peterson, *Only the Ball Was White* (Englewood Cliffs: Prentice-Hall, 1970); Roger Kahn, *The Boys of Summer* (New York: Harper and Row, 1971).

5. Bill James, *The Bill James Historical Baseball Abstract* (New York: Villard Books, 1986).

6. Seymour, *Baseball: The Early Years*, vii.

7. *Ibid.*

8. David Voigt, *American Baseball*, 3 volumes (University Park PA: Pennsylvania State University Press, 1983).

9. Since this essay was originally written, Seymour added a third volume to his history of baseball, which dealt precisely with these issues. See Harold Seymour, *Baseball: The People's Game* (New York: Oxford University Press, 1990).

10. I have limited the topic of this review essay to book length monographs dealing with the major leagues or Negro Leagues. I have deliberately avoided the general histories of Seymour and Voigt, which, with the exception of volume three of Voigt's work, predate the 1980s. A comparison of their work is worth a separate essay in itself. I have also declined critical comment on my own book, *Baseball's Great Experiment: Jackie Robinson and His Legacy* (New York: Oxford University Press, 1983). I will leave it to others to decide if I have met the criteria that I have defined here. Finally, I have omitted several books that deal only partially with baseball. See, for example, Gunther Barth, *City People: The Rise of Modern City Culture in Nineteeth-Century America* (New York: Oxford University Press, 1980) and Melvin Adelman, *A Sporting Time: New York City and the Rise of Modern Athletics, 1820–1870* (Urbana: University of Illinois Press, 1986). Adelman's discussion of baseball in the pre-major league era is outstanding.

11. Steven A. Riess, *Touching Base: Professional Baseball and American Culture in the Progressive Era* (Westport CN: Greenwood Press, 1980).

12. Stephan Thernstrom, *Poverty and Progress: Social Mobility in a Nineteenth-Century City* (Cambridge: Harvard University Press, 1964).

13. Riess, 221.

14. Richard C. Crepeau, *Baseball: America's Diamond Mind, 1919–1941* (Orlando: University Presses of Florida, 1980).

15. See, for example, Henry Nash Smith, *Virgin Land: The American West As Symbol and Myth* (Cambridge: Harvard University Press, 1950) and Leo Marx, *The Machine in the Garden: Technology and the Pastoral Ideal in America* (New York: Oxford University Press, 1964).

16. Crepeau, xi.

17. *Ibid.*, 21, 23, 48, 176, 217.

18. *Ibid.*, 91, 124.

19. Seymour, *Baseball: The Early Years*, 3.

20. Ralph Andreano, *No Joy in Mudville: The Dilemma of Major League Baseball* (Cambridge MA: Schenkman, 1965), 46.

21. Lee Lowenfish and Tony Lupien, *The Imperfect Diamond: The Story of Baseball's Reserve System and the Men Who Fought to Change It* (New York: Stein and Day, 1980). An updated version of *The Imperfect Diamond* published by DaCapo in 1991 carried the story through the 1980s.

22. Peter Levine, *A. G. Spalding and the Rise of Baseball: The Promise of American Sport* (New York: Oxford University Press, 1985); Eugene Murdock, *Ban Johnson: Czar of Baseball* (Westport CN: Greenwood Press, 1982).

23. Levine, ix.

24. Andreano, 56. Levine's analysis is quite similar to Andreano's, though

apparently he was unfamiliar with *No Joy in Mudville*. Neither his footnotes nor bibliography cite Andreano.

25. Levine, ix–xiv.

26. Murdock, ix–xii.

27. Charles C. Alexander, *Ty Cobb* (New York: Oxford University Press, 1984).

28. *Ibid.*, 6, 24.

29. *Pittsburgh Courier*, September 18, 1948.

30. Robert Peterson, *Only the Ball Was White* (Englewood Cliffs: Prentice-Hall, 1970).

31. Seymour remedied this situation with a long section on blacks and baseball in *Baseball: The People's Game*, but given the chronology of his earlier two volumes and the organization of the third volume, this subject appears as more of a side show than an integral part of the history of professional baseball.

32. Carl T. Rowan with Jackie Robinson, *Wait Till Next Year* (New York: Random House, 1960).

33. Camden House in South Carolina reissued this classic in 1983. The University of Nebraska Press published a new edition, edited by Jerry Malloy, in 1995.

34. Andrew S. "Doc" Young, *Great Negro Baseball Stars and How They Made the Major Leagues* (New York: A. S. Barnes, 1953).

35. Jackie Robinson, *Baseball Has Done It* (New York: Lippincott, 1964).

36. Roy Campanella, *It's Good to Be Alive* (Boston: Little, Brown, 1959).

37. Leroy "Satchel" Paige and David Lipman, *Maybe I'll Pitch Forever* (New York: Doubleday, 1962).

38. Willie Mays and Charles Einstein, *Willie Mays: My Life In and Out of Baseball* (New York: Dutton, 1972); Henry Aaron, as told to Furman Bisher, *Aaron, r.f.* (Cleveland World Publishing, 1968).

39. Jack Orr, *The Black Athlete: His Story in American History* (New York: Pyramid Books, 1970).

40. Peterson, *Only the Ball Was White*.

41. Cited in Donn Rogosin, *Invisible Men: Life in Baseball's Negro Leagues* (New York: Atheneum, 1983), 67.

42. John Holway, *Voices from the Great Black Baseball Leagues* (New York: Dodd, Mead, 1975). See also Holway, *Bullet Joe and the Monarchs* (Washington DC: Capital Press, 1984); Holway, *Smokey Joe and the Cannonball* (Washington DC: Capital Press, 1985); and Holway, *Blackball Stars: Negro League Pioneers* (Westport, CT: Meckler Books, 1988).

43. Bill Heward and Dimitri V. Gat, *Some Are Called Clowns: A Season with the Last of the Great Barnstorming Teams* (New York: Thomas Y. Crowell, 1974).

44. William Brashler, *Bingo Long and His Traveling All-Stars and Motor Kings* (New York: Harper & Row, 1973).

45. For an excellent example see Theodore Rosengarten, "Reading the Hops: Recollections of Lorenzo 'Piper' Davis and the Negro Baseball League," *Southern Exposure* (1977), 62–69.

46. Art Rust, Jr., *Get That Nigger Off the Field* (New York: Delacorte, 1976).

47. Effa Manley and Leon Hardwick, *Negro Baseball... Before Integration* (Chicago: Adams Press, 1976). Quincy Trouppe, *20 Years Too Soon* (Los Angeles: Sands Enterprises, 1977).

48. William Brashler, *Josh Gibson: A Life in the Negro Leagues* (New York: Harper & Row, 1978).

49. Several nonacademic works are also worth mentioning. James A. Riley produced a Who's Who of Negro League play, *The All-Time All-Stars of Black Baseball*, which profiled several hundred athletes who had appeared during the Jim Crow era. (TK Publishers, 1983). See also Jerry Malloy, "Out at Home," *The National Pastime* (1983), 14–28; and Malloy, "Black Bluejackets," *The National Pastime* (1985), 72–77 for two important works about blacks and baseball outside of the Negro Leagues.

50. Tygiel, *Baseball's Great Experiment*.

51. Rogosin, *Invisible Men*.

52. Janet A. Bruce, *The Kansas City Monarchs: Champions of Black Baseball* (Lawrence: University Press of Kansas, 1985).

53. *Ibid.*, 3, 44, 66, 127.

54. Rob Ruck, *Sandlot Seasons* (Urbana and Chicago: The University of Illinois Press, 1986).

55. Subsequent authors have amply fulfilled this promise. For a list of recent books on the Negro Leagues, see note 2 in "Unreconciled Strivings: Baseball in Jim Crow America," in section 2 of this collection.

TEN

Sports from a Sofa

Benjamin Rader. *In Its Own Image: How Television Has Transformed Sports.*
New York: Free Press, 1984. ix + 228 pp. Bibliographical essay and index.
$15.95.

On May 17, 1939, several hundred people gathered at the RCA building in
New York City to witness the first baseball telecast. The game originated at
Columbia University's Baker Field, but within the studio it appeared on a
small black and white screen, which made the players look "like white flies"
and obscured the course of the ball on all but infield plays. *New York Times*
correspondent Orrin E. Dunlop reported, "Seeing baseball on television is
too confining, for the novelty would not hold up for an hour, if it were
not for the commentator," but nonetheless marveled at the very idea of
"baseball from a sofa!" (pp. 17–18).

Given the primitive nature of this first sports telecast and the embryonic
status of television itself, perhaps none of the observers envisioned the
manner in which this new medium would transform the world of American
sports. Over the next four and a half decades, however, as Benjamin Rader
argues in his readable and provocative history of the marriage of these two
American institutions, "Television has had a large impact on the ethos of
sports; on the motives and behavior of the athletes, owners, and spectators;
and on the organization and management of sports. In turn . . . the changes
induced by television have altered the role that sports play in American life"
(p. 3).

It is difficult for even the most ardent sports fan of the 1980s to con-
jure up the sporting universe at the dawn of the television era. In the
professional realm, only baseball among the team sports, and boxing among
the individual competitions, had broad followings. Football and basketball
remained largely collegiate phenomena, the professional leagues forging a

marginal existence in midwestern industrial towns and a few large cities. Sports like golf and tennis attracted the participation and attention of a slim elite sector of the populace, while gymnastics, swimming, and track and field (even in the form of their quadrennial Olympic celebration) evoked only passing interest by current standards.

The geography of baseball, the undisputed "national" pastime of the age, illustrates the athletic provincialism of pretelevision America. The major leagues consisted of only sixteen teams (compared to the current twenty-six) playing in eleven cities, with St. Louis, hosting the Cardinals and the Browns, representing both the southernmost and the westernmost locale. Thus, as Rader points out, the vast majority of American baseball fans saw legendary figures like Babe Ruth or Joe Dimaggio only in "the fertile recesses of [their] imagination" (p. 2). It is small wonder that during the postseason months, when major league all-star teams barnstormed through the small cities and towns of the nation, their visits evoked a holiday atmosphere as schools and businesses closed, and people flocked to the ballpark to see the demigods they had heard so much about. Or, that minor league baseball, ranging from Class AAA to Class D level, became a central cultural component of hundreds of American communities.

The advent of television, writes Rader, unraveled this long-standing pattern. With major league baseball available to virtually every American household (by 1956, reportedly 75 percent of all homes had televisions) minor league attendance plummeted from a high of forty-two million in 1949 to only fifteen million in 1957 and ten million in 1969. Minor leagues faded from the landscape, as more than 60 percent of the fifty-one circuits ceased operations between 1949 and 1970. Other victims of the television age included the barnstorming tours and, to some extent, the Negro Leagues, both of which disappeared with hardly a trace by the early 1960s. At the major league level, the quest for higher television revenues weakened the bonds of team and community, as franchise after franchise forsook their traditional bases for broader media markets.

The transformation of baseball was perhaps the most visible mani-festation of what Rader calls "The Great Sports Slump of the 1950s," a malaise created not only by television, but "a revolution in the ways that Americans had begun to spend their spare time." As part of the suburban thrust of the post–World War II era, Americans shifted from "inner-city, public forms of recreation to private, home-centered forms of recreation" (p. 33). Television, the new focal point of the American living room, also became the centerpiece of this "privatization of leisure." Confronted by competition from a myriad of home-based activities, attendance at virtually all major sporting events (as well as other forms of entertainment) declined precipitously.

At the same time the mutual courtship of sports and television began in earnest. The symbiotic relationship between the media and athletics, however, was not new. Rader, whose 1983 text ranks as the best single-volume history of American sports,[1] traces the alliance from its nineteenth-century origins, when newspapers like the *New York Herald* and magazines like the *National Police Gazette* discovered that they could boost circulation not only through sports coverage, but by the actual promotion of athletic events. Pioneer radio entrepreneurs of the 1920s and 1930s duplicated the earlier cooperation (over the misguided objections of many team executives fearing diminished attendance), successfully broadening the national sports audience.

In the 1950s sports programming offered a convenient and inexpensive way for fledgling television stations and networks to fill airtime. The arena sports of boxing, wrestling, and roller derby, with their limited and localized action, became staples of the early years of television. The boxing mania grew to such proportions that local stations offered matches featuring seven- or eight-year-old boys or women combatants. In each instance, the sport was tailored to meet the perceived needs of the television audience with an emphasis on greater action and entertainment extraneous to the actual contest. In boxing the need to present "only winners" greatly depleted the ranks of the professionals, almost destroying the sport. By the end of the decade the romance had worn off and telecasts of the arena events declined. In a precursor to later developments, argues Rader, when these sports surrendered their authenticity, fans lost interest and tuned in to alternative offerings.

Not until the 1960s, however, was the true potential of sports telecasting realized, first by the tight-knit cartel of National Football League owners led by Commissioner Pete Rozelle, and second by network executives at the American Broadcasting Company, most notably the canny Roone Arledge. For NFL owners, many of whom had struggled to keep their marginal enterprise alive since the 1920s, television provided the rewards they had long hoped for. Color images, instant replays, and isolated cameras enhanced the presentation of the game and both popularity and television royalties soared. In 1956 CBS paid slightly over one million dollars for the annual rights to NFL games; eight years later this figure jumped to fourteen million dollars. Attempting to end the CBS monopoly, ABC subsidized the new American Football League with a five-year forty-two-million-dollar contract. By 1970 the two leagues had merged and contracts with all three major networks generated over fifty million dollars in revenues each year, a figure which has more than tripled to date. The cornerstone of this lucrative arrangement is the annual Super Bowl, which, in the short span of less than two decades, Americans have elevated to a *de facto* national holiday.

While football reaped the major benefits among the professional ranks, ABC introduced Americans to "the joy of victory and the agony of defeat" at the amateur level, simultaneously demonstrating the ability of sports programming to build overall network ratings. Rader is at his best in chronicling the rise of ABC from the third-ranked network to the preeminent television outlet, as a result, in large part, of its expanded sports coverage. After a decade characterized by an almost total absence of major athletic events, in 1959 ABC began a profitable alliance with the Gillette Safety Razor Company, which sponsored a rejuvenated "Fight of the Week" program and made possible NCAA football telecasts. Using Gillette money, ABC Sports Director Roone Arledge offered viewers golf tournaments and a variety of Amateur Athletic Union events—the basis for the widely praised and emulated "Wide World of Sports." The Arledge philosophy was "to get the audience involved emotionally. If they didn't give a damn about the game, they might still enjoy the program" (p. 106). Under his stewardship, ABC transformed the Olympic Games into one of the nation's ultimate sports passions, in addition to making it one of the great vehicles for promoting ABC's prime-time fare. Arledge capped these feats by introducing professional football and Howard Cosell to a Monday night audience, modifying the viewing and living habits of half the nation.

To Rader, the impact of these developments has been almost uniformly negative, not only for sports, but for American society. "Before the advent of television," he writes, "Americans usually experienced sports as a unique form of human drama" that "offered a wonderful release from everyday life." Our games "enacted familiar ceremonies that reaffirmed society's core values." Today, he argues, this has changed. "Television has sharply attenuated the traditional sporting experience" by "destroying the distance between fan and athlete," thus reducing "the ability of sports to elevate athletes into heroes." "With its enormous power to magnify and distort images . . . television has sacrificed much of the unique drama of sports to the requirements of entertainment," leading to rule changes that emphasize action over strategy and surrounding the games with "external intrusions" that have "contaminated" the "authenticity of the sporting experience." As a result, television has "diminished the capacity of sports to furnish heroes, to bind communities, and to enact the rituals that contain and exalt society's traditional values" (pp. 4–6).

The existence of such television "trashsports" as "Battle of the Network Stars" and the "Celebrity Battle of the Sexes" attests to the validity of Rader's eloquent and amply illustrated critique. Yet, at times, Radar exaggerates and thus weakens his case. His evocation of sports in the pretelevision age often reflects an ideal, rather than an actual, state of affairs, while his accounts of the modern era overemphasize the damage that television has done to our current games. Rule changes that add offense to the major sports, such as the designated hitter in baseball or the three-point play in basketball, reflect not simply the demands of the television audience, but also the evolutionary nature of modern athletics.[2] Contrary to their usual portrayal, franchise shifts to larger market areas represent less the heartlessness of corporate athletics than the demographic realities of post–World War II America. Although it pains this Brooklyn native, the transcontinental migration of the Dodgers has long since proved beneficial to both baseball and the nation. The transfer of teams to western and southern cities have made professional sports more truly national and expanded the opportunities for spectators to witness these events.

Nor is it clear that sports in the television age serve a less unifying role. Did Brooklyn Dodger pennants mean more to the community than the triumph of the 1969 Mets or the 1982 Super Bowl victory of the San Francisco 49ers? Rader cites the 1951 Dodger–Giant playoff as the quintessential "shared experience" of the earlier era. But far more people saw and identify with the famous Pittsburgh Steeler "immaculate reception" of 1972 or the classic sixth game of the 1975 World Series.

Indeed, television's greatest contribution has been the democratization of spectator sports. In exchange for the "purity" of our earlier games, television has provided greater opportunities for Americans to enjoy the finest athletes in this nation and the world, in a far broader variety of sports than ever before possible. This, however, does not negate Rader's accomplishment. *In Its Own Image* combines the burgeoning fields of sports and television history and raises critical questions that scholars and students of American popular culture must ultimately deal with.[3] As the literature in these areas expands, Rader's analysis will likely shape the contours of the emerging debate.

NOTES

1. Benjamin Rader, *American Sports: From the Age of Folk Games to the Age of Spectators* (1983).

2. See, for example, Allen Guttman, *From Ritual to Record: The Nature of Modern Sports* (1978).

3. Other, less scholarly, forays into this area include William O. Johnson, Jr., *Super Spectator and the Electric Lilliputians* (1971) and Ron Powers, *Supertube: The Rise of Television Sports* (1984).

ELEVEN

Ken Burns Meets Jackie Robinson

There is no denying the accomplishments of Ken Burns's *Baseball*. The eighteen-and-a-half-hour documentary created an unprecedented oral and visual history of the game and brought it before a broad audience of both devout fans and the uninitiated. Throughout the week that the series aired, I was repeatedly approached by people—many of whom had no previous interest in baseball—who were religiously and enthusiastically viewing the spectacle. Yet, while recognizing Burns's achievement, I was deeply disturbed by many aspects of the series. To demonstrate my qualms, I will analyze Burns's treatment of the subject that I know best: the saga of Jackie Robinson and the racial integration of baseball. The decision to focus on Burns's depiction of Jackie Robinson, reflects not only my own area of expertise, but the importance of Robinson and racial equality to the entire *Baseball* series. Burns repeatedly stated that the issue of race was the central theme of his work and the "Sixth Inning" episode was the pivotal juncture of his documentary. Certainly, here he would take great pains to ensure accuracy.

The segment begins with former baseball commissioner Happy Chandler's marvelous rendition of "Take Me Out to the Ball Game" and recounts the familiar tale of Jackie Robinson breaking the color barrier in major league baseball. Although Burns adheres to the fundamental spirit of the story, he takes substantial liberties with its sequence, facts, and events. The saga begins in spring 1945 as Brooklyn Dodger president Branch Rickey plans his historic breakthrough. The narrator, John Chancellor, describes a secret ballot wherein major league owners voted 15–1 against racial integration. But the discussion of this incident is problematical. While the owners' rejection of Rickey is a staple of the Robinson legend, there is controversy over whether a formal vote ever actually took place. If indeed it did, it occurred not in 1945, where Burns implicitly places it, but in August 1946.

The timing is significant. Rickey had not yet announced his plans in spring 1945. By August 1946, Robinson had already emerged as a star in the International League, and his promotion to the majors was imminent. Thus, Rickey in his planning was not, as Burns implied, bucking any clearly defined opposition from his fellow owners from the start. By the time the unified owners made their objections known (if indeed they did), Rickey's coup was a virtual fait accompli. Burns's historically misleading presentation was, obviously, based on a filmmaker's belief that the story worked better the other way.

The story then shifted to the charming recollections of Buck O'Neil, Negro League veteran and former manager of the Kansas City Monarchs, who described an incident that took place when Robinson played for that team. The Negro League club pulled its bus into a Southern gas station, where it hoped to fill the tanks and purchase food. When the station owner refused to serve the individual players, Robinson allegedly announced that they would purchase their gas elsewhere, whereafter the owner, fearful of losing the sale, capitulated. "We" learned a valuable lesson from Robinson, O'Neil indicated.

The gas station incident is a wonderful tale, repeated in many variations by former Monarchs to demonstrate Robinson's fiery temperament, his refusal to accept discrimination, and his awareness of the chinks in Jim Crow's armor. O'Neil's version appears authoritative. Viewers can only conclude from his presentation and reputation as Monarchs' manager that he was an eyewitness to these events. Yet, O'Neil, who was in the Army in 1945, never played with or managed Robinson on the Monarchs.

Such misrepresentations are presented throughout the Robinson segment. The narrator notes that after Robinson hit .387 in the Negro Leagues, *Pittsburgh Courier* sportswriter Wendell Smith arranged a tryout with the Boston Red Sox. The tryout, however, occurred in April 1945, *before* Robinson played for the Monarchs. Former Dodger scout Clyde Sukeforth described how he was sent to check out Robinson's arm and, if he liked how he threw, to arrange a meeting with Rickey. Moreover, according to the storyline, Sukeforth liked Robinson's arm and brought the two men together. The reality was more complex. Robinson had a sore arm when Sukeforth contacted him and was unable to throw or play. Sukeforth, who never saw Robinson play, took a gamble and set up the meeting anyway.

The initial 1945 tête-à-tête between Rickey and Robinson is part of American folklore. Burns has Sukeforth, the sole eyewitness to the conclave, describe it, while he focuses in on a still photograph of Ebbets Field. The camera closes in on the old ballpark, coming to rest on a particular window. The implication is unmistakable—Rickey and Robinson met, if not in this room, then at least somewhere in Ebbets Field. In fact, they met several miles away at the Dodger offices on Montague Street in downtown Brooklyn.

Burns repeatedly misrepresents photographs in a similar manner. When discussing the announcement of Robinson's signing with the Montreal Royals on October 23, 1945, Burns shows a photograph of Rickey signing Robinson to a contract. Rickey, however, was not at the Montreal signing ceremony (of which there are numerous photographs available). Burns's photo, taken several years later, has the advantage of showing Rickey and Robinson together, but has nothing to do with the historical events presented to the viewing audience. Likewise, Burns uses a dynamic filmstrip showing Robinson batting, fielding, and throwing bases while wearing a uniform with number twenty on the back and emblazoned with the word Royals on the front in 1946, when in truth, the sequence depicts Robinson as a member of the Kansas City Royals postseason touring squad in October 1945—not during his triumphant season with Montreal.*

Such "minor" gaffes aside, Burns sometimes blatantly distorted the historical record. For instance, in describing Robinson's 1947 season with the Dodgers, he recreated an incident in which Kentucky-born Pee Wee Reese—in the face of hostile taunts from Cincinnati players—placed his arm around Robinson's shoulder and silenced the abusers. There are many accounts of this incident but most, including Robinson's own recollections, place it not in Robinson's inaugural season, but in Boston in 1948. Similarly, later in this segment, the narrator describes Satchel Paige throwing a shutout in his first major league start on August 13, 1948. But Paige had previously started a game ten days earlier (after appearing in relief eight times), allowing three runs en route to a victory—not as dramatic as a shutout, but not bad for a forty-two-year-old rookie.

How serious are these errors? Burns has, perhaps correctly, dismissed his critics as "nitpickers," since individually none of the individual flaws are terribly significant. Yet, collectively, they reveal a disturbing pattern of manipulation and distortion that, if present in a literary history of these

---

*As a result of this gaffe, when the Montreal Expos retired Robinson's Royals uniform number in 1997, they retired number 20, instead of his actual number, which was 9.

events, would be clearly unacceptable. Burns, in his defense, distinguishes between the scholarly and the popular, the documentary and the literary. "First and foremost, know that I am a narrative historian," he told the *Journal of American History*. "I am interested in telling stories, anecdotes . . . creating a moment. . . . You place your audience there, or you do the best possible job of evoking what it must have been like." Burns considers himself "primarily an artist," and invokes the element of license. "As filmmakers," he informed another interviewer, "we were forced to take a certain amount of poetic license," based on available photographs and movies.

Given the paucity of visual evidence, some errors are trivial and even understandable. But, in other instances where Burns has a choice between accurate images and those he deems more dramatic, he invariably selected the latter. Often, he treated the factual record the same way, transposing events to create what he apparently believed to be a better narrative—making a distinction between "what it must have been like" and what really happened. This might be more palatable if Burns consistently accepted this distinction between history and art. But Burns attempts to have it both ways. Throughout the tireless promotion of his series and in response to his critics Burns repeatedly invoked his "distinguished panel of advisors who have been involved at every stage of the production" and his "Hall of Fame fact checkers [who] checked everything twice," claiming both accuracy and legitimacy for his work.

But not all documentary filmmakers grant themselves so much artistic license. According to historian James Green, who worked as a consultant on *The Great Depression* series, filmmaker John Else instructed his staff, "Everything should be what the audience believes it to be. We must adhere to a rigorous standard of accuracy, especially when borrowing from fiction to structure well-told documentary stories with drama, resolution, tragedy, and humor." Burns apparently operates under a different creed.

When asked about the furor over the errors in Ken Burns's *Baseball*, *Sporting News* archivist Steve Gietschier responded, "There are things in there that are misleading to people who are sticklers for historical accuracy. But the larger question is, is it important?" I leave that question to the readers.

TWELVE

The Polo Grounds

I first experienced the Polo Grounds in its afterlife. It was no longer what writers in the 1910s dubbed "the eighth wonder of the world"; nor was it the "opera house and the fighting cockpit of the golden age of Sports" of the 1920s, or even the inspirational site of Bobby Thomson's 1951 "Shot Heard 'Round the World" or Willie Mays's miracle catch in the 1954 World Series. The Polo Grounds in 1962 more resembled, according to a *Sporting News* headline, a "Torpedoed Ship That Refuses to Sink," or, in the words of Roger Angell, a "doomed old stadium." Given up for dead after the Giants had moved to San Francisco in 1958, the Polo Grounds had won a brief reprieve from demolition with the arrival of the New York Mets. While New York City built a new pleasure palace in Flushing Meadows, the fledging Mets would cavort in the well-worn arena on the banks of the Harlem River in upper Manhattan.

For a thirteen-year-old Brooklynite, little more than a month removed from his bar mitzvah, the trek to the Polo Grounds on April 27, 1962, marked yet another rite of passage. I had attended baseball games before—at Ebbets Field, where the Dodgers had celebrated my baseball baptism by hitting three ninth-inning home runs to defeat the Phillies 6–5, and at Yankee Stadium, where Mickey Mantle and Ted Williams had welcomed me with titanic home runs—but on those occasions my father had accompanied me. Now Robert Dorin, one full month my junior, and I were to attend our first ball game unescorted and unsupervised, newly anointed young men unleashed into the urban wilderness. The journey itself tested our adolescent mettle. We boarded the Remsen Avenue bus en route to the Utica Avenue station, where we caught the IRT Seventh Avenue subway. At Forty-second Street in Manhattan, we transferred to the D train on the Independent Line and traveled north to 155th Street, where we climbed the stairs to Eighth Avenue in the shadow of the looming stadium.

I have read that during the Met years, the Polo Grounds emanated the familiar signs of urban decay: peeling plaster, loose chunks of masonry, soot-blackened passageways, and cockroach-ridden lavatories. "It was like some ninety-year-old person suffering from arteriosclerosis," wrote Harold Rosenthal in *The Sporting News*. I don't remember it that way. The Polo Grounds possessed for me the same magical quality that all ballparks radiate: the silver-plated turnstiles that respond to a brisk forward movement, the vaulting ceilings and wide ramps of the entryways, the dark tunnels leading to the stands, and the sudden, irrationally unexpected, green expanse of outfield.

Robert and I purchased grandstand seats. In a modern arena the grandstand, if it existed at all, would place us in the far reaches of the upper deck. At the Polo Grounds we found ourselves in the front row in right field, less than three hundred feet from home plate, almost touching the players gathered beneath us during batting practice. We saw another schoolmate, Arnie Schurz, nearby. Before we had even settled in, a fly ball came soaring our way, dipped over the fence past Arnie's outstretched hand, caught him flush on the chest, and dropped to the ground. A horde of youngsters scrambled unsympathetically around Arnie's feet until one emerged with the ball, while Arnie rubbed his chest, dismayed more at losing the souvenir than at his discomfort.

The game itself, as recreated from the scorecard that Robert has faithfully kept for thirty-seven years, proved a representative sampling of the Mets' play in 1962. The Mets started their ace pitcher Roger Craig, who would lose twenty-four games that year, two other former Dodgers (Charlie Neal and Don Zimmer), and a couple of onetime major league stars (Richie Ashburn and Gus Bell). By the middle of the second inning, Craig was gone and the Mets trailed the Phillies 5–0. Catcher Hobie Landrith, the Mets' first pick in the expansion draft that had stocked the team ("You've got to start with a catcher or you'll have all passed balls," explained manager Casey Stengel), already had three passed balls. After the top of the sixth, the Phillies led 11–1. Then a remarkable transformation occurred. In the sixth the Mets scored three runs. In the eighth they scored four more. Heading into the bottom of the ninth, the score stood at 11–8. The Phillies hurler quickly retired the first two batters, but rookie pinch hitter Jim Hickman singled and then stole second base. Neal singled to drive in Hickman, making the score 11–9. This brought the potential tying run to the plate.

Although neither Robert nor I realized it, we were witnessing a characteristic Met moment. The trademark of the 1962 Mets, writes Leonard

Koppett, was "the futile rally. . . . They would fall far behind, rally to close the gap and come within sight of a tie or victory—and fall short." To the plate strode veteran utility infielder Don Zimmer. He had not had a hit that day. Indeed, he had not had a hit all season. He began his career as a Met with no hits in his first thirty-four at-bats. With Neal prancing off first and our youthful hopes high, Zimmer struck out to end the game. Many baseball fans have never forgiven Zimmer, who to date in 2000 has spent five decades in the game, for his mismanagement of the Boston Red Sox in the 1970s. I have never forgiven him for frustrating my naive expectations in 1962. Within three weeks Zimmer would be gone, traded for a left-handed pitcher named Bob Miller (not to be confused with a right-handed pitcher named Bob Miller who also pitched for the Mets that year). Catcher Landrith, who failed to fulfill Stengel's passed-ball prophecy, had also departed, traded for a legend-to-be-named-later, Marvelous Marv Throneberry.

During the next two seasons, I spent many happy days and evenings at the Polo Grounds, blithely impervious to its shortcomings, blissfully suffering through the Mets' misadventures. The ballpark sat in Coogan's Hollow, a narrow expanse of land sandwiched between the Harlem River and a massive outcropping of mica schist (known as Coogan's Bluff) that loomed over the structure. King George I of England had granted the land to John Gardiner in the eighteenth century, and the Gardiner manor house had sat on the bluff. In the late nineteenth century, James J. Coogan, a Bowery upholsterer with Tammany Hall connections, married into the Gardiner family and gave his name to the property. Coogan became Manhattan's second borough president in 1899. His family would own the bluff, hollow, and stadium into the 1960s.

In the 1880s the New York National League baseball franchise had played its games on a tract bordered by Fifth and Sixth Avenues and 110th and 112th Streets in Manhattan. Previously the land had hosted polo games, and the area became known as the Polo Grounds. In 1889 the city government announced plans to complete 111th Street and bisect the park. Giants owner John Day looked northward to the outskirts of the city and built a new ballpark at Coogan's Hollow. To avoid confusion and attract the faithful, he carried the name Polo Grounds to the new site. The following year, however, labor troubles rent the National League as most of its stars bolted to form their own Players' League. The New York franchise also leased land at Coogan's Hollow and built Brotherhood Park alongside the new Polo Grounds. So close were the two arenas that fans in one park could watch the game in the other. Hemmed in by Coogan's Bluff on one side and the National League facility on the other, Brotherhood Park adopted an elongated, horseshoe shape with a distant center field and short foul lines. Nonetheless, the Players' League stadium was by far the superior field. When the uprising collapsed after the 1890 season, National League owner Day insisted that as part of the settlement he be allowed to move his Giants from the new Polo Grounds to Brotherhood Park, which, to be consistent, he renamed the Polo Grounds.

The Giants remained in their new home for twenty years. After 1903, behind the leadership of John McGraw and the pitching of Christy Mathewson, they became the dominant franchise in the National League. The Polo Grounds, however, like most stadiums built in the nineteenth century, had been constructed entirely of wood. In the early morning hours of April 14, 1911, a night watchman saw flames engulfing the right center field stands. By the time firemen arrived in their horse-drawn equipment, the fire had consumed all but a small section of the outfield bleachers, destroying the third version of the Polo Grounds.

John T. Brush, who now owned the Giants, vowed to replace the old wooden structure with a modern concrete and steel facility to match those already in place in Pittsburgh, Chicago, and Philadelphia. In the latter two cities team owners Charles Comiskey and Ben Shibe had named their new arenas for themselves. In New York, Brush envisioned, a magnificent new amphitheater, the largest in the major leagues, to suit the nation's greatest city. He would call it Brush Stadium. The fans, however, from the moment it opened on June 28, 1911, with Christy Mathewson shutting out the Boston Braves, called the new ballpark the Polo Grounds. After 1919, when the Stoneham family bought the team, the Brush imprimatur faded from memory. The Stonehams also renovated the ballpark in 1923, creating the arena of most common memory.

Most people associate the Polo Grounds with baseball (and especially the New York Giants, its primary occupants), but during its half century of existence, the venerable ballpark witnessed a wide, and often improbable, assortment of spectacles. In April 1912 the Giants and the crosstown Highlanders (soon to be renamed the Yankees) held an exhibition game to benefit the survivors of the *Titanic*. George M. Cohan and other celebrities sold programs and newspapers to raise funds. During World War I, Isadora Duncan danced at the Polo Grounds during a war bonds rally.

In the 1920s the Polo Grounds emerged as a primary showcase for the golden age of sports. The Yankees had made the Polo Grounds their home since 1913. Thus, when Babe Ruth arrived in New York in 1920, he alighted not in Yankee Stadium, which would not be built until 1923, but at Coogan's Hollow. Indeed, the Polo Grounds added to Ruth's sensation. The Babe's unprecedented home-run hitting in 1920 and 1921 owed much to the friendly dimensions of his new home. Playing with the Red Sox in 1919, he had hit only nine home runs at Fenway Park. He hit twenty-nine home runs at the Polo Grounds in 1920 and thirty-two in 1921. These totals tailed off when the Yankees moved to the Bronx. "I cried when they took me out of the Polo Grounds," confessed Ruth.

Since the Yankees and Giants dominated baseball in the early 1920s, the Polo Grounds became virtually synonymous with the World Series during those critical years. The arena played host to nineteen out of twenty-six World Series games between 1921 and 1924, including thirteen consecutive games in 1921 and 1922, when the Yankees and Giants both won pennants. The first radio broadcasts of the World Series occurred there in 1922, and pioneer baseball announcer Graham McNamee debuted at the Polo Grounds in 1923.

These years also established the Polo Grounds as a haven for college and professional football. The Army-Navy contest was held in the oddly shaped arena nine times between 1913 and 1927. On October 19, 1924, after sportswriter Grantland Rice watched Notre Dame defeat Army 13–7, he indelibly christened the Irish backfield the "four horsemen." Beginning in 1925, the New York Giants of the National Football League made the Polo Grounds their home. On one memorable 1925 weekend seventy thousand fans turned out to watch Army beat Navy on Saturday. On Sunday an even larger crowd literally stormed the stadium to see Red Grange debut as a professional football player. Fans scaled walls and crashed through locked gates to see "the Galloping Ghost," demonstrating the economic potential of the professional game for the first time. The football Giants would play their home games at the Polo Grounds for more than three decades.

The Polo Grounds also welcomed boxing in the 1920s. Eighty-two thousand fight fans posted the sport's first million-dollar gate to watch Jack Dempsey fight Luis Angel Firpo, "the Wild Bull of the Pampas," for the world's heavyweight championship in 1923. In the first round Dempsey and Firpo exchanged knockdowns. At one point a Firpo blow drove Dempsey through the ropes and into the press row. The referee delayed the count, allowing Dempsey to crawl back into the ring, where he devastated the Argentine challenger, winning in the second round. A second memorable heavyweight championship fight occurred in 1941 when an aging Joe Louis met Billy Conn. When experts predicted that the younger Conn, a deft strategist, might outmaneuver Louis in the ring, the champ responded,

"He can run, but he can't hide." After Conn dominated Louis for twelve rounds, Louis finally found him and knocked him out in the thirteenth.

At various times the Polo Grounds featured midget auto races, rodeos, soccer, tennis, rugby, lacrosse, trap shooting, dog shows, and ice-skating and skiing festivals, complete with ski ramps and snow. Religious rallies and opera graced the field. Ironically, no one ever played polo there.

In retrospect, it is hard to believe that the Polo Grounds ever existed in the twentieth century. With its odd configuration, unexpected hiding places, erratic angles, and eccentric nooks and crannies, it evokes more the ethos of a medieval castle or abbey, or perhaps an unexplored corner of Harry Potter's Hogwarts School for Witchcraft and Wizardry, than a modern stadium. The massive clubhouse in center field sometimes served as home to the baseball Giants owner Horace Stoneham, who often slept there. Stoneham also constructed an apartment under section thirty-five in the left field grandstand where groundskeeper Matthew Schwab and his family lived during the 1950s.

As Robert Creamer noted, "The Polo Grounds [was] a terrible place to watch a ball game." Although the stands officially seated fifty-five thousand people, half that number, Creamer observed, seemed to fill the park. In the upper decks, people in right field could not see the right fielder and people in the left field could not see the left fielder. Many seats were located behind the stadium's bountiful array of posts and pillars. According to Creamer:

> Some seats in the Polo Grounds are behind several posts simultane-ously, particularly those in the rear of the lower stands behind the dugouts. Watching a game from there is like watching it through a picket fence, and the people who sit there sway back and forth continuously during a game, first one way to get a glimpse of the pitcher winding up—as the batter disappears behind a post—and then the other way, abruptly dismissing the pitcher to watch the batter swing.

Even the field managers did not have an unobstructed view. Because the elevation of the playing surface dropped by eight feet between the infield dirt and the most distant fences, a manager seated on the bench could only see his outfielders from the waist up.

The horseshoe-shaped stands opened in center field, creating a unique, absurd, yet unforgettable configuration. The clubhouse loomed at a sixty-foot height in far distant center field, five hundred feet from home plate. Atop the structure sat a giant Longines clock. Along the top level a row of windows overlooked the field. A mammoth advertising billboard covered the bottom half of the clubhouse. In the Giants' heyday the sign advertised Chesterfield cigarettes, and the *H* or the *E* would light up in the brand name to indicate a hit or an error. During the Mets era, the clubhouse wall also functioned as a scoreboard, with a Rheingold beer sign providing the lighted scoring assistance. A wide runway leading to the clubhouse separated the two sections of bleacher seats. In the absence of underground tunnels, pitchers and other players removed from the game had to march the hundred-plus yards across the field, walk between the bleachers, and climb an open flight of steps to reach the clubhouse locker room, exposed to the cheers, or more often taunts, of fans throughout the extended journey.

The center field bleachers, arrayed on both sides of the clubhouse runway, consisted of long, narrow, uncomfortable slats of wood, officially holding 3,900 people. Since there were no specific seats, however, the capacity varied from game to game. The highest rows of the bleachers located people a distant six hundred feet from home plate. Even in the front sections, fans watching an errant play often experienced, as Arnold Hano wrote in *A Day in the Bleachers*, "the same miserable frustration of a man who watches a holdup but is too far away to warn the victim." Two square green screens, designed to provide a dark backdrop for the batters, blocked out the lower centermost seats in each section.

The Polo Grounds also offered an unusual vantagepoint for those who could not or would not pay for a ticket. Since the ballpark sat directly beneath Coogan's Bluff, fans could sit atop the mica escarpment and watch games for free. In the old wooden Polo Grounds, the grandstand ascended only halfway up the escarpment, offering a relatively full panorama of the game from the cliff, a nearby viaduct, or the elevated train. After 1911 the new ballpark yielded a more obstructed view. Fans atop the bluff could hardly see the pitcher, catcher, or batter and rarely either the right fielder or first baseman. The shortstop, left fielder, and center fielder, however, were in plain view, as was the second baseman on plays near the base and the third baseman when he cut in front of the shortstop. One could also see the big scoreboard above the center field bleachers.

The view became more cramped after the 1923 renovation when the Giants extended the grandstand, effectively cutting the shortstop and left fielder from the picture, and eliminating the scoreboard. The advent of public radios in the 1930s somewhat offset this disadvantage. Hano, who as a boy lived across the street from the Polo Grounds, remembered climbing the wooden stairs to the top of Coogan's Bluff. "There, with a scattered hundred other fans enjoying a sun bath, we'd watch the game," he recalled. "All you can see through the open work of the stadium is the rear portion of the pitcher's mound, the area around second base, and a portion of the outfield. But after awhile, you get the hang of it from the noise of the crowd and what the second baseman does." In the 1950s the completion of the Colonial Park Housing Project on the Harlem River Drive eliminated even more of the view. Nonetheless, Roger Angell discovered a crowd of about forty people clustered atop the bluff peering at "a slice of emerald grass in deep center field" and listening to their radios during a Mets-Dodgers game in 1962.

The most peculiar part of the Polo Grounds lay in the dimensions of the playing field itself. Its oblong shape placed the foul line fences dangerously close and center field and the power alleys dauntingly remote. The right field wall stood a scant 257 feet from home plate. The distance to the seventeen-foot-high left field barrier was calculated at 279 feet, but even this minimal measurement exaggerated its depth. Since the upper deck in left field featured a twenty-three-foot overhang, a pop-up hit a mere 250 feet could clip the edge of the stands and become a home run. Polo Grounds regular Hano recalled, "At least a dozen times I have seen this happen . . . the left fielder pressed against the fence as though he hoped to push back the stands to make room for the lazily dropping fly ball, and then the gentle smiting of the facade and the ball lying innocently at the feet of the left fielder, while the batter runs around the bases, sometimes hesitating at second base as though not sure he had actually hit a home run."

Balls rocketed to center field usually suffered an opposite fate. The power alleys in left and right center field were so deep that they housed the bullpen and warmup areas for both teams unprotected by any screen or barrier. The center field bleachers languished almost 450 feet away. The runway between the two bleacher sections added another fifty feet of playing area. Even the clubhouse, over five hundred feet distant and sixty feet high, remained in play. No line demarcated the height above which a blast would be deemed a home run, but then again no batter ever reached the clubhouse on a fly.

Few men ever hit a ball into the bleachers. Visiting National Leaguer Spud Davis once hit a ball off the screen, but only legged out a double for his efforts. In 1948 Luke Easter of the Negro League Homestead Grays become the first man to clear the center field fence during a game. Five years later a ball hit into a gale wind by Milwaukee Brave Joe Adcock carried eight rows up into the stands. Easter and Adcock remained the only hitters to reach the bleachers until 1962, when the Mets occupied the premises. In the first inning of a game on June 17, Lou Brock, a slender, left-handed rookie Chicago Cubs outfielder, came to the plate. Brock would play eighteen years in the majors, averaging a scant eight homers a season. Yet on this day he unexpectedly drove a ball into the right-side section of the bleachers. The following day the Braves came to town. Before the game someone pointed out where Brock's shot had landed to Henry Aaron. Aaron stared at the far-off fence as if measuring it in his mind. Several innings into the game he stepped up to bat with the bases loaded and lifted a Jay Hook pitch over the fence into the opposite sector of the bleachers from where Brock's blast had landed. Thus, on consecutive days in their third month of existence, the Mets surrendered more home runs into the Polo Grounds bleachers than the Giants had in over thirty seasons.

Nonetheless, fans better remember the Polo Grounds for its long outs than its mammoth home runs. In the 1922 World Series Babe Ruth hit a ball a reported 480 feet on the fly only to have it caught by Giants center fielder Bill Cunningham. Fourteen years later in the sixth game of the World Series, with the Yankees needing just one out to win the championship, Hank Lieber of the Giants smashed a ball into straight-away center into the gap between the bleachers. Joe DiMaggio glided under the ball and caught it at the base of the clubhouse steps. Without breaking stride he started up the stairs and had ascended to the clubhouse before many fans had realized that the series had ended.

The most remarkable demonstration of Polo Grounds perversity occurred on an October afternoon in 1954 when the Giants met the Cleveland Indians in the first game of the World Series. In the top of the eighth inning, with the score tied and fleet-footed Indians runner Larry Doby on second base, Vic Wertz drove a high arcing drive into deep right center field. Giants outfielder Willie Mays wheeled and took off in pursuit of the ball. The photographs of the play capture a classic juxtaposition of determined player and expectant fans. Mays has his back to home plate, his arms outstretched toward the fence, his number 24 flashing defiantly. The bleachers host a diverse ensemble of men (but few women). A policeman leans forward next to the stairs leading to the clubhouse. The head of a young boy barely peers over the barrier. Two men desperately grasp the screen at its rightmost extension. A vendor holds a soda frozen in midair, watching the action before finishing his service. A handful of African Americans are seated in the front row; others are sprinkled throughout the crowd. Most white fans are dressed in sport shirts and have bare heads. The blacks, continuing the traditions of Negro League fandom, wear sport jackets and hats. All have their eyes fastened on Mays.

Hano, seated in the bleachers, described the moment: "Mays was turned full around, head down, running as hard as he could . . . Mays simply slowed down to avoid running into the wall, put his hands up in cup-like fashion over his left shoulder, and caught the ball much like a football player catching leading passes in the end zone." Equally miraculous, Mays instantaneously whirled and heaved the ball toward second base, falling flat on his stomach from the effort. Doby had tagged at second base after the catch, intent on taking two bases and scoring the go-ahead run. But Mays's Herculean throw arrived in the infield just as Doby reached third, preventing his further advance and preserving the tie.

Two innings later, in the bottom of the tenth, Giants pinch hitter Dusty Rhodes lifted a gentle fly over the head of the Cleveland first baseman. Second baseman Bobby Avila dashed out, thinking that he might have a chance to catch the drifting fly ball. Right fielder Dave Pope eased backward, settling under the ball. Suddenly he felt the intimate right field fence at his back as the ball continued to float. Pope stretched his glove upward and leaped as high as he could, but the ball cleared the wall, bouncing off a front row seat and back onto the field at Pope's feet. Wertz's long, fruitless out had traveled more than 420 feet, Rhodes's game-winning home run less than 300. No other ballpark could have produced so unlikely an outcome. The Giants went on to sweep the World Series in four games.

The Giants had now played in the Polo Grounds for more than forty years. The age of John McGraw, during which the Giants had won eight pennants in their first fourteen seasons there, had drawn to an end in 1932 with the team uncharacteristically languishing in the second division. McGraw's successor, player-manager Bill Terry, revitalized the club into a World Series winner in 1933 and won a pair of pennants in 1936 and 1937. Left-handed slugger Mel Ott, who feasted on the short right field fence, led Terry's Giants. Memorably lifting his right leg high as he swung, Ott hit 323 home runs at home, but only 188 on the road. In the twilight of his career in 1943, he hit eighteen home runs, all of them at the friendly Polo Grounds.

The decade after 1937 was a fallow one for the Giants, but in 1948 owner Horace Stoneham shocked the baseball world by luring longtime Brooklyn Dodgers manager Leo Durocher to Coogan's Bluff to assume the helm of the Giants. Durocher's arrival ushered the Giants into the golden age of New York City baseball. Between 1947 and 1957, a New York City team appeared in nine of the eleven World Series. Seven times the Series pitted the Yankees against either the Dodgers or Giants. Often the Dodgers and Giants competed bitterly for the National League pennant.

The high point of these challenges came in 1951, when Durocher drove his squad from thirteen-and-a-half games back in August to catch the front-running Dodgers at the season's end, forcing a three-game playoff. The Giants narrowly won the first game, 3–1, but the Dodgers roared back to win the second 10–0. The third and final game pitted Dodgers ace Don Newcombe against Giants standout Sal Maglie. The Dodgers took a 1–0 lead into the bottom of the seventh, but the Giants tied the game on a sacrifice fly by third baseman Bobby Thomson. In the top of the eighth, the Dodgers seemingly broke the game open with three runs against Maglie. They led 4–1 going into the bottom of the ninth inning. Three Giants hits, however, made the score 4–2 and drove Newcombe from the mound. Dodgers manager Charlie Dressen brought in pitcher Ralph Branca to face Bobby Thomson with two Giants on base. Thomson drove Branca's second pitch on a line toward the left field fence. The ball was hit so hard and straight it did not need the benefit of the famed overhang. It dropped into the lower left field stands about a dozen feet above the head of left fielder Andy Pafko, who stood forlornly at the wall. The Giants had indeed won the pennant, in perhaps the most famous game in baseball history.

The intense Dodger-Giant rivalries assumed an added significance against the backdrop of the breaking of baseball's color line. Jackie Robinson had joined the Dodgers in 1947. In 1949 the Giants added former Negro League stars Monte Irvin and Hank Thompson to their roster, becoming the second National League team to integrate. In 1951 the two teams between them fielded seven of the league's eight black players, including rookie sensation Willie Mays. The dramatic playoff confrontation posed a compelling argument that even the most hard-line racists among major league owners found difficult to rationalize against or ignore, paving the way for more widespread integration.

The 1951 playoffs and 1954 World Series marked the last hurrahs for the Polo Grounds of the Giants. Over a million people came to watch Mays and his teammates in their 1954 championship season. But the ballpark, now four decades old, had begun to atrophy, and the neighborhood around it suffered from crime and decay. Robbers accosted fans, and on one occasion a bullet fired from a nearby rooftop killed a spectator during a game. Built to take advantage of mass transit lines, the Polo Grounds suffered from woefully inadequate parking. As the Giants dropped in the standings, attendance plummeted along with them. In 1956, after thirty-one years of residency, the football Giants announced they were moving to Yankee Stadium. Rumors floated that when the Giants' lease expired in 1962 the old ballpark would be torn down and replaced by a low-income housing project. On June 18, 1958, Giants owner Horace Stoneham announced,

"We can anticipate a decrease in income each year from now on. . . . As a fan and president, I know the Giants must leave the Polo Grounds." Two months later, Stoneham confirmed that the Giants would leave New York and go west to San Francisco.

On September 29, 1957, the Giants played their last game at the aging arena. Eleven thousand fans turned out to watch the veterans of the 1951 and 1954 pennant-winning teams—Mays, Thomson, Rhodes, and others—lose 9–1 to the Pirates. At the game's end souvenir-seeking fans ravaged the field, ripping up bases, pitching rubbers, signs, and telephones. John McGraw's widow, Blanche, disconsolately watched the final game. "I still can't believe I'll never see the Giants in the Polo Grounds again," she exclaimed. "New York can never be the same to me."

"Dispossessed" groundskeeper Matty Schwab and his family moved out of their left field apartment, but the old ballpark retained some vitality. Jay Coogan, whose family still owned the land and stadium, vowed, "The Polo Grounds will not be demolished quickly. I will wait for callers. I am not going to give up." In 1958 the Polo Grounds hosted Israel's tenth anniversary celebration, a rodeo, Gaelic football, and a series of Sunday baseball games featuring the remnants of the Negro Leagues. The next few years also saw professional soccer come to the Polo Grounds. The New York Titans of the new American Football League assumed occupancy in 1960, although owner Harry Wismer called the park a "graveyard" and, according to one sportswriter, most of the fans came disguised as empty seats.

In 1962 the Mets moved into the arena for a planned one-year stay. On the last day of the season, they staged a fond farewell to the Polo Grounds. Television cameras caught septuagenarian manager Casey Stengel, who had played many games at the ballpark in the teens and twenties, slowly walking from home plate to the remote clubhouse as "Auld Lang Syne" filtered through the loudspeakers. Once again, however, the reports of the Polo Grounds' demise had been greatly exaggerated. When problems delayed the opening of Shea Stadium, the Mets found themselves back in their crumbling castle in 1963. "At the end of the season they're gonna tear this place down," Stengel told home run–prone pitcher Tracy Stallard as he removed him from a game. "The way you're pitchin' that right field section is gone already."

But even in New York City construction projects inevitably reach completion. The Mets and the Titans, now renamed the Jets, moved into Shea Stadium in 1964. On April 10 of that year, the long-scheduled destruction of the Polo Grounds began. Employees of the Wrecking Corporation of America, bedecked in Giants shirts, repeatedly slammed a two-ton iron "headache ball," the same ball that had demolished Ebbets Field in Brooklyn, against the superstructure of the Polo Grounds, reducing the once grand sports palace to rubble. Four thirty-story apartment buildings, dubbed Polo Grounds Towers, rose on the site. On the patch of land once occupied by the vast green acreage of center field sits an asphalt playground. They call it Willie Mays Field. To date, no one has played polo there.

THIRTEEN

Salaries Are Escalating, but
They Don't Guarantee Winning

Legendary baseball executive Branch Rickey reigned in the golden age of baseball management. "It was easy to figure out Mr. Rickey's thinking about contracts," remarked Chuck Connors, who played for the Brooklyn Dodgers before moving on to a more lucrative career as television's Rifleman. "He had both players and money—and just didn't like to see the two of them mix."

Modern baseball executives, on the other hand, at least a select few of them, have lots of money and seem intent on throwing it at players. The Texas Rangers shelled out $252 million to secure the services of shortstop Alex Rodriguez for the next decade. The Boston Red Sox anteed up $160 million for eight years' worth of outfielder Manny Ramirez.

These signings, the mind-boggling totals notwithstanding, make at least a modicum of sense. Rodriguez, at the modest age of twenty-five, when most ballplayers enter their prime years, has already established himself as perhaps the greatest shortstop of all time. Ramirez, twenty-eight, has driven in 632 runs over the past five seasons.

But, as maverick owner Bill Veeck commented in the early years of free agency, one rarely overpays a superstar; it's the cost of the supporting cast that most often proves crippling. How, for example, can one explain the $55 million paid out by the Los Angeles Dodgers for pitcher Darren Dreifort? Dreifort, it's true, was the second choice in the 1993 amateur draft, taken just behind Rodriguez. Unlike A-Rod, however, he has yet to fully deliver on his potential. He has never won more than thirteen games in a season, never recorded an earned run average below four, never thrown two hundred innings or struck out two hundred batters in a season.

Time may ultimately prove this a wise investment for the Dodgers. The perennial shortage of even modestly talented pitchers clearly placed a premium on Dreifort's value. The Colorado Rockies reportedly offered him

$60 million to hurl in Coors Field, a perennial pitchers' graveyard. Dreifort, already wealthy beyond most people's wildest dreams, judiciously turned down the extra millions to toil in the friendlier confines of Dodger Stadium. Nonetheless, $55 million remains a remarkable reward for a twelve-game winner.

My usual approach to baseball salaries is to ignore them. They are, or should be, a private matter between owner and player. I should be no more interested in Dreifort's income than he is in mine. Since free agency became a reality in 1975, every bump up the salary scale from Reggie Jackson's $600,000 a year in 1976 to A-Rod's $25 million in 2001 has evoked cries of ruin and desolation from baseball Cassandras. Yet, baseball's popularity has grown steadily (when not interrupted by strikes) and spectacularly in the age of free agency. Cable television has enhanced baseball's marketability, and per-game attendance has more than doubled between the 1970s and 1990s. Nor, despite anecdotal evidence to the contrary, do fans seem to balk at paying higher ticket prices, especially when the money goes to winning teams or those playing in new stadiums.

Yet, the recent splurge in salary spending has raised more substantial issues. Has the division between baseball's haves and have-nots accentuated to the point where only a handful of very wealthy teams can afford the best talent and contend for the pennant? Has the game evolved to the point where the majority of low-income teams, like the Montreal Expos, are doomed to fail before their lackluster hurlers even fire their first pitch?

The history of baseball yields little support for the proposition that a fundamental change has overtaken the game. The greatest competitive imbalances occurred not since the onset of free agency, but during the era in which the reserve clause bound players to one team and gave owners the upper hand in salary negotiations. Between 1921 and 1968, the Yankees won twenty-nine American League pennants in forty-eight seasons; the Giants, Dodgers and Cardinals accounted for thirty-four of the National League championships in this span. In most of these years, teams like the Phillies, Athletics and Senators had less hope of reaching the World Series than the Expos do today. Ironically, free agency, which many feared would lead to domination by wealthy teams, had exactly the opposite effect. Between 1976 and 1993, nine different National League teams and ten different American League teams won pennants.

Many believe, however, that the post-1995 emergence of a new Yankee dynasty heralds the dawn of a new age of competitive imbalance. The Yankees, who boast the highest revenues and largest payroll in the major leagues, have won four World Championships in five years. Their opponents in three of these series, the Braves in 1996 and 1999 and the Mets in 2000, also rank among baseball's economic elite. Furthermore, the Yankees have now presumably paved the way to more pennants by signing former Baltimore Oriole pitching ace Mike Mussina to a long-term contract. Surely, argue many observers, including Commissioner Bud Selig, the baseball situation has reached crisis proportions and the game's future is in dire jeopardy.

This may well be true, but the evidence is less than conclusive. The current Yankees may be no different from earlier dynasties, like the Cincinnati Reds of the 1970s or the Oakland A's of the late 1980s. A strong farm system, shrewd trading, and excellent personnel decisions—in short, wise management—has played at least as large a role as excess revenue streams in the Yankee success. Nor has a dynasty emerged in the National League, where four different teams have reached the World Series in five years.

Certainly, having ample revenues is an advantage. But the Chicago Cubs have the third-highest TV income in baseball, and no one has seen them in the World Series in more than half a century. The Dodgers and Orioles indiscriminately dole out multiyear, multimillion-dollar contracts and accumulate lavish payrolls, but neither team has parlayed their extraordinary largess into a pennant in recent memory.

Indeed, the results of the 2000 campaign, the ultimate Yankee triumph notwithstanding, point to the most evenly balanced competitive baseball universe in decades. For the first time in major league history, no team in either league had a winning percentage exceeding .600 or a losing percentage under .400. While the Yankees staggered to victory in the American League East, the Chicago White Sox and Oakland A's, teams at the bottom end of the salary scale, won the Central and Western Divisions. The San Francisco Giants triumphed over their more profligate rivals in the National League West.

The Yankee example perhaps proves that deep pockets and sound management may be an unbeatable combination. The courtship and signing of Dreifort, however, gives hope to underfunded franchises and their fans. Rickey explained good fortune in baseball and in life with the adage, "Luck is the residue of design." He might have added the following corollary: No amount of luck can overcome a flawed design, no matter how much money you spend.

Acknowledgments

Introduction to *The Jackie Robinson Reader: Perspectives on an American Hero.* New York: Dutton, 1997.

"The Court-Martial of Jackie Robinson." *American Heritage*, July/August 1984, 34–39.

"Jackie Robinson's Signing: The Untold Story," with John Thorn. *Sport*, June 1988, 65–70.

Afterword to *Baseball's Great Experiment: Jackie Robinson and His Legacy.* Expanded ed. New York: Oxford University Press, 1997.

"Black Ball: The Jim Crow Years." In *Total Baseball: Official Encyclopedia of Major League Baseball*, ed. John Thorn, Pete Palmer, and Michael Gershman. 7th ed. Kingston NY: Total Sports Publishing, 2001.

"Unreconciled Strivings: Baseball in Jim Crow America." In *Past Time: Baseball as History.* New York: Oxford University Press, 2000.

Introduction to *It's Good to Be Alive,* by Roy Campanella. Lincoln: University of Nebraska Press, 1995.

"Black Ball: The Integrated Game." In *Total Baseball: Official Encyclopedia of Major League Baseball*, ed. John Thorn, Pete Palmer, and Michael Gershman. 7th ed. Kingston NY: Total Sports Publishing, 2001.

"Playing by the Book: Baseball History in the 1980s." *Baseball History*, winter 1986, 6–17.

"Sports from a Sofa." Review of *In Its Own Image: How Television Has Transformed Sports,* by Benjamin Rader. *Reviews in American History*, March 1985, 622–26.

"Ken Burns Meets Jackie Robinson." *Journal of Sport History*, spring 1996, 69–71.

"The Polo Grounds." In *American Places,* ed. William Leuchtenburg. New York: Oxford University Press, 2000.

"Salaries Are Escalating, but They Don't Guarantee Winning." *Los Angeles Times*, December 17, 2000.